DÉJÀVU

DÉJÀVU

John Osborne

faber and faber
LONDON · BOSTON

First published in 1991
by Faber and Faber Limited
3 Queen Square London WC1N 3AU

Photoset by Wilmaset Birkenhead Wirral
Printed in Great Britain by
Clays Ltd St Ives plc

John Osborne is hereby identified as author of this
work in accordance with Section 77 of the
Copyright, Designs and Patents Act 1988.

Applications for performance rights should be
addressed to Peters Fraser & Dunlop, 5th Floor,
The Chambers, Chelsea Harbour, Lots Road,
London SW10 0XF

A CIP record for this book is
available from the British Library

ISBN 0-571-14345-8

CLIFF: My feet hurt.
JIMMY: Try washing your socks.

Look Back in Anger

Keep thou my feet; I do not ask to see
The distant scene; one step enough for me.

I loved the garish day, and spite of fears
Pride ruled my will; remember not past years.

And with the morn those angel faces smile
Which I have loved long since and lost a while.

John Henry Newman

CHARACTERS

J.P.
CLIFF
ALISON
HELENA
TEDDY

AUTHOR'S NOTE

Look Back in Anger is bristling with stage directions, most of them embarrassingly unhelpful. I have tried to avoid them ever since. At that time, however, they were very necessary to an author if his intentions were to be approximated. Actors, indeed directors, demanded literal signposts, not only about motivation ('Why do I say this when I've just said the opposite?'), but where they should actually sit down. Those days are long gone ('Wryly. Moves left.'). But something must be said about J.P.'s speeches, especially the later ones. Sometimes, these achieve an almost stiff, calculated formality. This is quite intentional. They have the deliberateness of *recitative* and it may not be always easy to spot where the 'aria' begins. However, when these passages occur, they must be deft in delivery and as light as possible. J.P.'s particular artifice but casually knocked off. Read, memorize and discard.

Without wishing to place too many constraints on the interpretation of this part, it is nevertheless important to indicate what are tediously and popularly known as 'guidelines'. They can be observed without imposing too many restrictions on the actor's freedom of interpretation. The original character of J.P. was widely misunderstood, largely because of the emphasis on the element of 'anger' and the newspaper invention of 'angry young man'. The result of this vulgar misconception was often a strident and frequently dull performance. Wearisome theories about J.P.'s sadism, anti-feminism, even closet homosexuality are still peddled to gullible students by dubious and partisan 'academics'. They continue to proliferate and perpetuate themselves among those who should know better. J.P. is a comic character. He generates energy but, also, like, say, Malvolio or Falstaff, an inescapable melancholy. He is a man of gentle susceptibilities, constantly goaded by a brutal and coercive world. This core of character is best expressed, not only theatrically but truthfully, by a *mild* delivery. In other words, it is not necessary or advisable to express bitterness bitterly or anger angrily. Things should be delicately plucked out of the air not hurled like a protester's stones at the enemy. This was true of the original. It is even more appropriate to what might be thought of as *Look Back II*.

ACT ONE

The Midlands. The present. Sunday morning.

The large kitchen of a country house of the kind sometimes advertised as 'a minor gentleman's residence'. The kitchen itself retains its original farmhouse appearance of a working place at the heart of the building, dedicated to the pursuits of a large, prosperous and robust family. It is possibly the oldest part of the house with the original stone flags from an earlier period gleaming, leading off to a large butler's pantry, rooms for hanging game and preparing other fruits of the countryside. A few ancient hooks hang down from the high ceiling and a huge Aga dominates one side of the stage. All this workmanlike air of practicality has been modified in the interests of comfort, without too much emphasis on glossy Country Living. *In the suburbs the result would probably be described as a 'dinette'. However, it has rather evolved as a sitting room and kitchen, a place for talk and conviviality.*

A warm glow from the Aga niche gives out a comforting light from its engine-room-sparkle surface. A large, empty dog basket with its scatter of hairy blankets spilling out from it stands beside the stove, together with a sporting gun and cartridge belt. Upstage, large, floor-length windows look out to a distant park-like landscape with hills of pasture and forest beyond it. The right stage area is separated by a partition through which the actors can see and speak to each other. But the centre is the main working area, containing two large deep sinks, not too overwhelmed by smart kitchen embellishments of the magazine 'farmhouse' style. In short, a relaxing, not too functional place, certainly not 'high-tech', in which to gossip idly while peeling the potatoes or drawing a game bird.

The walls of its cupboards and discreet 'units' are covered with old postcards and quite cunningly lit. A few sporting prints and posters decorate other walls. A wooden, rough table, which serves both for dining and working, dominates the centre area, flanked by a couple of extremely bright and comfortable old armchairs. There is also a seasoned bench and rocking chair, a Windsor chair or two. On one

I

wall hangs a large Victorian-style sampler with the words: THANK
YOU FOR NOT SMOKING. *Nearby is another:* THOU GOD SEEST
ME.

As the curtain rises, ALISON, *a girl of about twenty, is leaning
over a well-used ironing board, upstage left. She wears a T-shirt
with the legend:* I AM SCUM. *In the two armchairs, right and left
respectively,* J.P. *and* CLIFF *are seated. All that we can see of them
is two pairs of legs, sprawled way out beyond the spread of
newspapers which hide the rest of them from sight. Beside them and
between them is a table on which sits a scruffy teddy bear, also
surrounded by a jungle of newspapers and weeklies.*

When we do eventually see them, we find that J.P. *is a grey-
haired man of indeterminate age, casually and expensively dressed.
Clouds of smoke fill the room from the pipe he is smoking.* CLIFF,
*the same age, is similarly dressed, perhaps slightly less Jermyn
Street.*

*The only sound is the occasional thud of Alison's iron on the
board. It is a chilly, grey February morning, with occasional shafts
of sunlight piercing the room from the french windows.*

J.P.: (*From behind newspaper*) What ho, Bernardo!
   (*Pause. Presently,* J.P. *throws his paper down and looks
   around. Nothing happens. He waits, listens, stares at Cliff's
   upraised paper hiding his face, then leans forward.*)
   What ho, Bernardo!
   (*No one responds.* J.P. *pauses then picks up his paper and
   disappears behind it again. Silence.* ALISON *pauses, looks at
   the two armchairs, pushing back the hair from her face. She
   goes to a transistor radio beneath one of the cupboards stage left
   and turns it on. After a little expert fiddling, the machine
   responds with a loud blare of pop music. She glances across to
   the men, then turns the volume down to a level which most sane
   people would think quite loud, and returns to the ironing board,
   where she carries on at her task with a little more relish. There
   is no response from the other two occupants for a while. Then
   J.P. lowers his paper and listens. Slowly and deliberately he
   gets up, goes over to the transistor and turns it off. He looks at
   ALISON, who smiles sourly and puts on headphones. Looking to*

2

CLIFF *for a reaction, he returns to his chair, picks up his paper and disappears behind it once more. The room remains silent except for the clatter of Alison's iron. Presently, his papers are set down again as he relights his pipe. Smoke pours from it as he clamps it down into a steady burn and he returns cheerfully to behind his paper.* ALISON *begins coughing. Pause.* CLIFF *sets down his paper and stares at the papers from which heavy clouds are rising.* ALISON *coughs again.* CLIFF *looks as if he might be about to protest, then retreats again behind his own paper. Silence as before until* J.P. *puts down his paper even again, looking round him. Then:*)

Why *do* I do this every Sunday? (*Pause.*) I keep thinking it's Friday.

CLIFF: Well, it's Sunday.

J.P.: *La paix du dimanche.*

CLIFF: What's that?

J.P.: Some cunning French play I expect. All bombast and logic and no balls.

CLIFF: You don't say. Did you know that . . .

J.P.: What?

CLIFF: Yesterday was St Valentine's Day.

J.P.: Oh, yes.

CLIFF: Nary a card on the mat for me, matie.

ALISON: I sent you one.

CLIFF: Oh, that's nice.

ALISON: Perhaps it'll come tomorrow.

CLIFF: That's very thoughtful, Alison.

J.P.: She's very thoughtful. Tardy perhaps.

CLIFF: Something to look forward to.

J.P.: Well, it's time you looked forward.

CLIFF: Shouldn't we all.

J.P.: I used to dread tomorrow. Now it's only today.
   (*Sings softly:*)
      Woke up this mornin', hopin' the day wouldn't come
      Woke up this mornin', but it wouldn't go away.

CLIFF: Blind Lemon Porter again.

ALISON: Blind who?

J.P.: In bed last night, got the blues about today

3

Woke up this mornin', but it wouldn't go away.

CLIFF: That's Sunday for you.

J.P.: Now there's tomorrow.

CLIFF: Sure is, whitey.

J.P.: Now there's tomorrow, can't find yesterday.

CLIFF: You surprise me, man.

J.P.: Woke up this mornin', so tired and young and grey.

CLIFF: Well, you do look *dated*, but still powerful, man, still powerful.

J.P.: Wait for the evening, still feelin' younger . . .
      Hopin' tomorrow . . .

CLIFF: . . . will go away.

J.P.: . . . won't be no worse than today . . .

CLIFF: Where's my Valentine?

J.P.: Teddy sent you one.

CLIFF: Unstamped no doubt.

J.P.: That crimson twilight won't chase the blues away.

CLIFF: No more crimson twilight, colonel. No more blues. Try soul.

J.P.: What's that?

CLIFF: Ask your daughter.

J.P.: Here! Yesterday. Prig's Own Paper too among the ads for Community Creative Projects Directors. (*Picks up another paper.*) Here: six full pages. It's here somewhere, a pulsing little message of pretending unrequited, shameless love. Senior Race Officers . . . Yes. Ah. Piggy Poos sends Kissy Poos to Mummy Piggy Poos and Curly Wigglers to Twirly Piglets.

CLIFF: Snuffle Bum wants Cuddle Drawers ever so ever and always Kentish Town Snuggle Wumti-Tumkins.

J.P.: All graduates and Harvard men.

ALISON: Here's one opposite the Court Circular. Naughty Boy Wittgenstein must have Mummy Meanie Winkle. Always, always, always.

CLIFF: Twinkle Twinkle Teggy Twinkle
      How I love your Ursine Twinkle.

J.P.: That sounds like Teddy.

CLIFF: If it is, it's to himself.

J.P.: That figures, I suppose.

ALISON: Bonky Potty What's must have you know what's. Kiss, Kissy Lobbergub Kissicles.

CLIFF: Flabby Love Wobble Hips all our Relationships.

ALISON: Squirrel's Drey Rent Free always and everwill for scruffy old bears. Please keep my paws and I will warm yours evermore.

CLIFF: Oh – my own gorgeous gusset.

J.P.: That – is enough nausea.

CLIFF: I do so agree. Teddy's quite nauseated. Whimsy.

J.P.: Kentish Town's made of harder stuff than that.

CLIFF: Well, yes, it is rather hard to believe.

J.P.: Well, it isn't *explained*, is it?

CLIFF: Palpably. Wouldn't have gone down in our day.
(*They resume papers.*)

J.P.: Grown-up persons. Most embarrassing.
(*Pause.*)

CLIFF: Snuffle Bum, Cuddle Drawers.

ALISON: Ugh!

J.P.: Ugh.
(*Pause.*)
Pour me some more wine, Whittaker, will you?

CLIFF: Pour it yourself.

J.P.: You're the nearest.

CLIFF: You're the oldest.

J.P.: Quite.
(CLIFF *pours him some more.* J.P. *sips it thoughtfully.*)
I don't feel so hot.

CLIFF: Now that won't do.

J.P.: No.

CLIFF: You've had a bottle and a half to yourself.

J.P.: The wine is excellent. Reticent, most despised of virtues, but *au fond* . . .

CLIFF: . . . *au fond* . . .

J.P.: Cheeky, subversive and coarsely voluptuous.

CLIFF: So what is it, don't tell me, colonel, friend o' mine?

J.P.: Brain fag.

CLIFF: Oh yes. Rather appropriate for you.

ALISON: Yes. Fags on the brain.

CLIFF: Exactly. Fags. Cigarettes, tobacco smoke, sodomites, brain, atrophy.

CLIFF *and* ALISON: Brain fag!
(*They both laugh.*)

J.P.: Such a droll pair. The executive echelons of television were rough hewn for the likes of you, Whittaker. How wise you were to take my advice and go in for that director's course when the Town Hall Praesidium took away our street trader's licence all those years ago. (*To* ALISON) He told the BBC he'd fallen off the back of a lorry, which they took to be an example of quirky Welsh wit, didn't they?

CLIFF: That's right, boyo.

J.P.: Boyo. Listen to the Shepherd's Bush woodnotes wild. For thirty-seven years I have listened to that wheedling half-back, Bible black, mother's Methodist pride warble. Are you going to talk like that for the rest of your life?

CLIFF: Well, I always have.

J.P.: I thought I'd got you out of it.

CLIFF: That was a most uncalled-for remark.

J.P.: You're right. *No* one called.

CLIFF: Teddy thinks it's uncalled for.

J.P.: Don't – don't hide behind Teddy. Nobody asked him (*to* TEDDY) did they? *I* know the inflexions, cautious, crafty and respectable. Do you know what his mother said when she returned from the put-upon pit wives' excursion to Florence on the coach?

CLIFF: Oh, God!

J.P.: 'Well, what did you think of the excursion to Florence, Mrs Lewis?' 'Oh, it was lovely. The coach ride was lovely. All the brown ale, the crisps and the singin'.' 'But what about Florence?' 'Florence?' 'Yes.' 'Oh, that. Well. I think. Well . . . A lot of thought's gone into it.'

CLIFF: You're being very condescending.

J.P.: Of course.

CLIFF: And predictable. And – sneering. Sneering and predictable.

J.P.: You used to be just agreeably offensive. His wife, poor

6

dear Ellie, may the Good Lord in his everlasting chapel
cheerfulness bless and keep her for taking this principality
front-parlour mouse off my hands for so long.

CLIFF: (*To* ALISON) He does have a way with the Celtic
cadence, doesn't he?

J.P.: Do you remember, you smart-arse media Welshperson?

CLIFF: In his clumsy fashion. Do you think Lord Sandy should
have been an actor? A lot of people thought he was. Now,
there's even a hint of *hiraeth*, pit-pony Porter,
masquerading as a nature's thoroughbred.

J.P.: You never had style, nor invention, brain dead to
spontaneity . . .

CLIFF: Mind you, he's half Welsh himself.

ALISON: I know.

CLIFF: Born in Monmouth. Now that used to be in England.

J.P.: Still is.

CLIFF: Well, the timetables on the platforms are in Welsh. Just
peeved because he can't read 'em.

J.P.: Well, I know the Welsh for 'May I please have a packet of
Daz?'

ALISON: What is it, then?

J.P.: (*Precisely*) *Am cwn amwrn dai llangollen barra kowse* –
packet of Daz! – There!

ALISON: Keep the English out of Wales.

CLIFF: Damn right. What have *you* done for Wales?

J.P.: Why do you imagine dear old Offa stuck his dyke up the
road. To keep you dark, hairy, pointy-hatted little buggers
out. Old Ellie's kept you in your pleased little place all
right.

CLIFF: (*To* ALISON) He makes it all up, you know. His
memory's over-revved. What is it, Lord Sandy?

J.P.: When you left me in our flat, lumbering me with our
flourishing, yes, flourishing sweet stall.

CLIFF: Leaving – his girlfriend moved in is what he means.

J.P.: I said – which you won't remember – some respectable
little madam from Pinner or Guildford would gobble him
up in six months.

CLIFF: Brits Out!

7

J.P.: I am *not* a Brit. I am English.

CLIFF: God's most divine gift.

J.P.: You bet. Nor do I exist or have my being in any tribal slum called the UK. I live among the hills footmarked only here, here, in ancient English time. No! It was Ellie who married *you*, sent you out to the studios, and here you are, clean as a Jermyn Street pin, all due to Ellie, not of Pinner or Guildford but Abergavenny, wartime prison of Rudolf Hess and neighbour to the founding saint of the National Health.

CLIFF: That rock on which our nationhood is built.

J.P.: Do you know what Ellie said the other day?

CLIFF: I wish she were here now.

ALISON: So do I.

CLIFF: T. S. Eliot and Pam. That act never really got off the ground.

J.P.: What are you on about?

CLIFF: Nothing, captain of my soul, nothing.

J.P.: Anyway, *she's* never heard of T. S. Eliot. They all did Elton John for 'O' levels. Wasn't it?

ALISON: Virginia Woolf, actually.

J.P.: Who else?

ALISON: She doesn't like him really.

CLIFF: Who – Virginia Woolf?

ALISON: Ellie. Him.

CLIFF: I don't think that's true.

ALISON: You just won't admit it – any of you, after a lifetime.

CLIFF: She's very fond of Lord Sandy.

ALISON: No, she's not. He upsets her.

CLIFF: No, he doesn't.

J.P.: (*American*) We have a little problem in communication as human beings but I'm sure you would agree that is one of the great dilemmas of our time. You and me, we have a communication problem in a number of areas, which are in urgent need of restructuring.

CLIFF: Meaning you don't like him either. Where does he get his resistible charm? His mother? I don't think so.

J.P.: She should be among us now. This world was fashioned

for the likes of her. Alas, she passed away peacefully, watching *Crossroads*, while the home help was helping herself to her handbag and a while before some thumb-brained sob sister dreamed up the miracle malady of hypothermia, an affliction unknown to her grandmother, who would as lief as died from a surfeit of lampreys.

CLIFF: Most unconcerned of you, I must say. (*To* ALISON) We had a different lifestyle in those days.

J.P.: Like we didn't use dumb words like 'lifestyle'. The pursuit of which is confined to those incapable of any style whatsoever.

CLIFF: Like myself.

J.P.: Just so. What I did know was what I did *not* want to grow up to be was a member of the public.

CLIFF: And you never did.

ALISON: Or the human race.

CLIFF: A palpable hit. On the behalf of yoof. You could have been like this woman. (*Newspaper*.)

J.P.: What woman?

CLIFF: This lady doctor. She's the country's leading expert on anal dilation in abused children.

J.P.: Quite. Think of the avenues that might have been opened up to you.

CLIFF: Or closed. Mind you, she does have a funny squinty-eyed look.

J.P.: Scarcely surprising. I may not be an identifiable or believable member of the public but at least I don't put my postcode on my writing paper.

CLIFF: Oooh! There *was* a time when you'd have said 'notepaper'. Still I won't let on. Besides, Ellie says we *must* use the postcode.

J.P.: Yes, well, we mustn't mess up the system. Ellie's right. Do you know what else she said on her last visit?

CLIFF: Must you?

J.P.: I asked her to sit down on that huge Regency sofa I bought, the one I've just had re-covered with such gorgeous originality. She sat on it very reluctantly, gave it a

9

sort of hopeless, intensive-care pat and said, 'Lovely . . . How will you keep it clean?'

CLIFF: Yes, and 'you *have* noticed there's a stain on the upper left-hand corner of the staff toilet?'

J.P.: I gave him, that misshapen object, that uppity Welsh nigger, the most exquisitely camp sweater last Christmas, the purest of white to play off his junk-clogged plebeian skin with an elegantly amusing motif –

CLIFF: Motif?

J.P.: He tried it on, and I must say it didn't look too bad, for the hobbled runty class-creature that he is. Went into Ellie to get her verdict and you know what she said? '*Lovely*, Cliff! Only thing is if you wear it, it'll get dirty.'

CLIFF: Well, it *was* too good to wear, it's true.

J.P.: Ah, the marriage of adventurous minds.
    (*Pause.*)

ALISON: I don't see what's so amusing about that.
    (*Pause.*)

CLIFF: What are you giving up for Lent?

J.P.: Um?

CLIFF: What are you giving up for Lent?
    (*Slight pause.*)

J.P.: Ethnic culture. And you?

CLIFF: The Alternative Service Book.

J.P.: You don't go to church.

CLIFF: Alternative comedy. Alternative women. Radio One. Oh, gay–lesbian *thé dansants*. It should be genuine deprivation.

J.P.: Very well. Donating to charity.

CLIFF: You don't.

J.P.: I used to . . . street barrel organists.

CLIFF: And you, Alison. What about you?

ALISON: The Prime Minister.

J.P.: And they say the young have no hope.
    (*They return to the newspapers.* J.P. *relights his pipe.* ALISON *grimaces as the clouds of smoke reach her. She waves at it in front of her face.*)

CLIFF: What do you suppose Teddy's giving up for Lent?

J.P.: Buggery.

CLIFF: Steady on, J.P. That's not a very Teddy sort of word.

J.P.: What *is* a Teddy sort of word?

CLIFF: Meaningful relationship, I suppose.

J.P.: Makes your eyes water, you mean?

CLIFF: You really shouldn't say things like that in front of him.

J.P.: Behind his back, whoops, sorry! That would be better?

CLIFF: You know how hurt he is by words.

J.P.: You mean the word 'buggery', but not the act?

CLIFF: Come on, Lord Sandy, you've more compassion in you than that.

J.P.: What about sodomy?

CLIFF: There's no talking to him in this mood. He's not really so unfeeling. Are you, you whimsical old softie?

J.P.: I'm only mildly curious. Is Teddy a sodomite or isn't he?

CLIFF: He's one of God's creatures and is entitled to dignity and respect from the likes of coarse ruffians like you.

J.P.: I've no disrespect for Teddy. He has all the charm of a Lithuanian carpet seller. I just wonder why he must wear his heart on his cock.

CLIFF: As you – even in your heartless bigotry – must know: he doesn't have one.

J.P.: Perhaps that's why he's given it up? Buggery, I mean.

CLIFF: Must you be so hurtful?

J.P.: Pricks and moans don't break his bones but words will hurt him ever? Don't you think it piquant –

CLIFF: Piquant! Oh, *yes*.

J.P.: Don't you think it piquant that a most devoutly illiterate generation should be so maidenly about the form of words?

CLIFF: He refuses to be humiliated by this glib stereotyping.

J.P.: Good for Ted.

CLIFF: It's reducing.

J.P.: Indeed. Reduce a stiff prick up the arse and, lo, no stereotype. Only the limp but meaningful truth. If it's so meaningful, why is he giving it up?

CLIFF: I didn't say he was giving it up. *You* did.

J.P.: Did I?

CLIFF: Yes. How do you know, anyway?

J.P.: I assumed.

CLIFF: Assumed! (*Almost losing his temper.*) Oh, great!

J.P.: That was why he's looking so bloody miserable. He's not getting it.

CLIFF: What?

J.P.: Buggered. Sorry, meaningful relationships.

CLIFF: He just objects to your unfeeling use of words.

J.P.: So I understand. He likes doing it but not hearing it.

CLIFF: Anyway, he's into safe sex.

J.P.: Safe sodomy? Like meatless steaks?

CLIFF: He's into Green. Why shouldn't he campaign for the Green way of life?

J.P.: Why not? Better to be Green than slouch unseen. Decaffeinated copulation.

CLIFF: He doesn't want penetration. Just stroking.

J.P.: Stroking. Like the Boat Race.

CLIFF: Like tender, loving, on-going relationships.

J.P.: I remember her.

CLIFF: Who?

J.P.: Penny.

CLIFF: Penny who?

J.P.: Penny Trayshun. Strong, muscular girl, full of merriment, built like a nutcracker. Like Poppy.

CLIFF: Poppy?

J.P.: Poppy Tupper.

ALISON: I'm going mad.

CLIFF: I'm getting confused.

J.P.: Demonstrably.

CLIFF: Let's drop Teddy and Lent, shall we?

ALISON: Hoo-bloody-ray.

J.P.: (*Presently, reading from the paper*) 'Speaking from his £200,000 bungalow, Roddy said: Debbie and me are in love and we want all the world to know it.' Did you know it?

CLIFF: I did actually.

J.P.: You do keep up with the world, don't you? 'I know people says I shouldn't have left my bride and young baby. And I'm thirty years older than she is . . .' Open another bottle of the '75, will you.

CLIFF: I'm too tired.

ALISON: I'll get it.

J.P.: Oh, thank you.

(ALISON *goes off*.)

'A spokesman for the Group said, Rod and Debbie are wildly in love. You only have to see them at the poolside, hammering away at it.'

CLIFF: Actually, someone in the village asked me the other day what you do for a living.

J.P.: Oh?

CLIFF: That nice woman with the strawberry mark in the ironmongers.

J.P.: And? What did you reply, dreamboat?

CLIFF: I just said, 'Oh, well, you'll know James by now, always a bit of an unsolved Jimmy Riddle.' 'Oh, a lot of people have got him taped, I expect,' she said. And she laughed.

J.P.: Well, next time tell her I'm better off ignored.

CLIFF: Oh, I think she'll do that.

J.P.: Good. I don't want to be summed up or identified. When I ran a sweet stall nobody believed *that*. Why should they believe me now?

CLIFF: Why. Indeed?

(ALISON *returns with a bottle of wine*.)

J.P.: Oh, you found it.

ALISON: '75. (*She starts to open it*.)

J.P.: (*Faintly surprised*) Oh, very kind . . . I think even I deserve a little better than to be explained.

(*Back to newspapers*.)

(*Presently*) You never really got it going as a mouse, did you?

CLIFF: No.

J.P.: Bit of a wash-out . . .

CLIFF: As a mouse – yes.

J.P.: You weren't really cut out for it.

CLIFF: Not really.

J.P.: Still – you had a go. That's the thing –

CLIFF: I wasn't convincing.

J.P.: Yet, you had recognizable mouse-like qualities. Alison thought so. We both did . . .

(ALISON *pours wine into his glass. He watches her.*)

And yet . . . I can think of people who have mouse-like qualities who are able to exploit them with enormous success, benefit and pleasure to everyone. (*To* ALISON) Thank you. Very nicely poured.

(ALISON *goes to fill Cliff's glass.*)

CLIFF: Oh, thank you, lovely.

J.P.: She poured that very nicely, don't you think?

CLIFF: She does everything nicely.

J.P.: You *were* embarrassing.

CLIFF: Deeply.

J.P.: Well, people used to get mighty hot over bears and squirrels – if they were exposed to that needless whimsy.

CLIFF: Ah, whimsy. It was.

J.P.: It *is*.

CLIFF: Ah! (*Holding aloft Valentine's Day paper.*) Prig's Paper. They have their cuddlesome community projects officers.

J.P.: What do you think, Alison?

ALISON: What's it matter what *I* think?

J.P.: You're the future, my dear bejeaned spokesperson, bristling with communication skills, and bearing down ever in the omnipresent.

ALISON: I think you both have a lifetime's inherited and laboriously perfected skill at talking untrammelled balls.

CLIFF: The fearless perception of yoof: that's what your daughter's got.

J.P.: She has. Give yourself a glass.

(ALISON *pours one.*)

Well, here's to us all. God bless this house and all within.

(J.P. *puts his arm round* ALISON.)

A glass of '75, the friendly sentinel of tobacco and loving company. What could be more agreeable? What we need is a song. Sing us a song, Alison. No, you don't sing or whistle, like your mother. Cliff? Well, I tell you what.

CLIFF: No, no more blues.

J.P.: As sung at champagne gatherings of pith and moment.

(He grabs pineapple from bowl on table, which he holds above his head. Dances and sings in the style of Carmen Miranda.*)

> I don't give a shit for Nicaragua,
> I don't give a bugger for Brazil,
> I don't give a hoot for Heethiopiaa,
> I'm the one the nobs would like to kill.

(J.P. tries to dance with ALISON.*)*

> I don't give a fart for Venezuela,
> I don't even know it on the map . . .

(ALISON breaks from him, back to the ironing board. He tastes his wine again.)

Actually, I believe some of the Venezuelan wines are quite drinkable.

CLIFF: Where did you pick up all these cheap tricks?

J.P.: Self-taught, my dear. Self-taught.

(J.P. sits down and returns to reading the paper.)

CLIFF: I feel quite snoozy.

J.P.: Well, don't go to sleep.

CLIFF: I see they're still having trouble in Market Harborough.

J.P.: Oh yes? Buttered toast.

CLIFF: What?

J.P.: Buttered toast. A recent survey carried out by the Human Engineering and Social Technology Department of Chichester New Town University has produced an impressive body of evidence in its third report that the annual consumption of more than five hectares of white buttered toast per person may lead to a serious incidence of pre-marital incest, particularly among young people.

CLIFF: They do seem to have trouble, some of these young people. I blame it on the teachers.

J.P.: And the parents. Why doesn't this government *do* something about it? Instead of raising up temples to the greater glory of greed and the sanctification of profitability, the blasting of the furry rights of helpless animals . . .

CLIFF: Man is born free but everywhere –

J.P.: Persons.

*An artist once endlessly impersonated by even the most humble drag queen.

CLIFF: – are crying buckets of Bollinger.

J.P.: A non-poly-saturated diet must be imposed by the process of education and, if necessary, by statute and, ultimately, other means. A national campaign must explain to the public the causes and dangers of buttered toast and the horrifying spectacle of the incest crisis about to shatter our English obsession with class. It cannot be too strongly repeated for the benefit of those young people unable to read the instructions on a used condom, that it cannot be caught by sharing a National Health dildo, inhuman cuts all absolutely no fear at all, as widely believed by the unteachable supine victims of a thousand unnatural governments that it cannot be passed by contact with a raised lavatory seat or any other infrastructure of a male-dominated political system or multiculture crisis situation.

CLIFF: Why has all this been kept from us for so long?

J.P.: Because, Whittaker, because our ancient freedoms and rights to expression are being slowly but inexorably strangled.

CLIFF: I thought it wasn't just my feet.

(*Pause.*)

There's an American academic here who thinks Shakespeare's a pretty ordinary writer.

J.P.: All blood's ordinary to a louse.

CLIFF: Teddy thinks he's overrated.

J.P.: Poor old W.S. How they hate him. Dumb bruins and pushy professors in soft jobs, guzzling in the armpits of a god. It must be irksome.

CLIFF: That's a good word. Shakespearean would you say?

J.P.: It will have to do.

(*Pause.*)

(*Suddenly*) A black feminist dike from Khartoum.

CLIFF: We *don't* wish to know that.

J.P.: A black feminist dike from Khartoum
        Took a nancy-boy up to her room . . .

CLIFF: We've heard it before, Alison?

J.P.: Well, *I* haven't.

A black feminist dike from Khartoum
Took a nancy-boy up to her room.
Here! Dear sir, as a severely handicapped and lifetime
campaigner for Fallen Sparrow Concern . . .

CLIFF: Fallen cuckoos for you, dear.

J.P.: Fallen Sparrow Concern, I feel I must protest most
vigorously against the unfeeling obsession and glorification
in your columns of the so-called properties of Kattomeat.
By doing this do you not realize that you are playing into
the ruthless paws of your own avowed persecutors and
enemies? The money being spent on this exploitative and
vile industry could go to providing a thousand kidney
machines and alleviate the sufferings of a million unsung
sparrows in the Third World. In this age of privatized
selfishness, is it not a scandal that some persons are sobbing
themselves to death in a sea of Perignon as they huddle,
Fidelio-like, and grieving beneath the aching spaces of the
river's span at Waterloo? A million nesting boxes cry out.
Take back your buttered toast. Take back your cardboard
box and – Give Me Yesterday.

CLIFF: The Château Concern '66, please, duckie, pass it over
here.
(J.P. *does so. Pause.*)
Did you know it was National Motivation Year?

J.P.: No.
(*Pause.*)

CLIFF: Apparently.

J.P.: Seems to have passed us by.

CLIFF: What?
(CLIFF *begins to nod. Pause.*)

J.P.: Lots of things. Don't go to sleep.

CLIFF: Why not?
(CLIFF *disappears behind the paper. Pause.*)

J.P.: (*To* ALISON) Nearly finished?
(ALISON *can't hear him.*)
Nearly finished?
(ALISON *nods.*)
You don't have to do that, surely? I thought ironing boards

were out of fashion when my first wife racketed about on them. Porter, J., on trumpet. Alison Porter on prayer book and ironing board.

(J.P. *looks at* ALISON *for a response. She is clearly absorbed in one of the Top Thirty or so*).

(*Presently*) Wouldn't you say that, Mr Interlocutor, madam? . . . Um.

(CLIFF'S *head has gone forward on his chest. Just dropping off.* J.P. *above him then leans forward above Cliff's slumped newspaper.*)

When you *wake* in the morning! –

CLIFF: (*Starts*) Stupid sod!

J.P.: (*Sings sweetly, slowly and very crisply, rather like Coward, to the tune of 'John Peel'*)

When you wake in the morning . . .

CLIFF: I'm going to bed . . .

J.P.: When you wake in the morning . . .
Full of . . . fucks and joy . . .
And . . . the wife's in prison . . .
And your daughter's coy . . .

(*Smiles at* ALISON.)

What's the matter with . . .

(*With emphasis*) The bottom . . . of your eldest boy . . .
When you wake . . . with the horn in the morning . . .

(CLIFF *looks at him, still rather dazed. Recedes behind paper for comfort.* J.P. *sups his wine. He smiles benignly at* ALISON.)

Songs for swinging sexists.

ALISON: Very nice.

J.P.: Well, you know, the Senior Citizens' Christmas outing. *They* like it. It cheers them up a bit. Me and Dorita find it gets them going.

CLIFF: Heigh ho.

ALISON: I was just thinking . . .

CLIFF: Now who sang that?

J.P.: My dear . . .

CLIFF: Webster.

J.P.: Oh yes. He could be amusing in those days.

18

CLIFF: Before success spoiled him.

J.P.: Success merely put the hollow crown on the hollow selfish shit he always was.

CLIFF: Wonder if he ever learned to play the banjo.

ALISON: Never mind.

J.P.: No, *please* . . . You were asking?

(ALISON *huddles back to her headphones.*)

ALISON: How did you really feel when Alison left you?

J.P.: How did I feel? Cliff?

CLIFF: How do *I* know what you felt?

J.P.: *You* were a witness to that memorable scene.

CLIFF: Well, go on, tell your little daughter. She's asked you a question. How did you feel when Alison left you?

J.P.: I felt . . . I thought . . . I shall never have to go to the ballet again . . .

(*They return to their papers.* J.P. *relights his pipe. It belches black and furiously around them.*)

You know what?

(*No response.*)

Well . . .

CLIFF: What?

J.P.: I *feel*. I feel: very Dayzhar Voo.

CLIFF: Yes?

J.P.: Yes.

(*Pause.*)

CLIFF: Dayzhar *what*?

J.P.: Dayzhar Voo.

CLIFF: Well, you always *were*, weren't you?

J.P.: Not really, people thought I was.

CLIFF: Get on. You were born *déjàvu*.

J.P.: Actually, you are quite wrong. As always and, impeccably, fashionably wrong, ignorant and deluded.

CLIFF: Now then, you should mind your rhetoric at your time of life. Sorry, Lord Sandy.

J.P.: Let me explain if I can penetrate the mists of your radical squalor. Our furry friend Teddy is *not déjàvu*, as you, and a million other clockwork cunts, would have it. Very simply because he is *not* something which you have 'already seen' –

19

literal translation from a forever foreign tongue. Thus, *déjàvu*. The meaning of which is quite simply the sensation of apparently recognizing some person or event which you could not possibly have ever witnessed. In other words, a deluded sense of recall, a *recherché* experience which could not have ever possibly taken place and most certainly not privy to the likes of canting pillocks like yourself.

CLIFF: My, that old White Tile Alma Mater did you proud, didn't it? Gave you a life-long grammar of aloofness.

J.P.: Indeed, but not, alas, the language.

(*Pause.*)

Do you remember the Bishop of Bromley?

CLIFF: Which one's that?

J.P.: Not the present one. The one who believed in God.

CLIFF: Oh yes. And the H-bomb. We rather liked him. Or did we?

J.P.: He was preferable to this one.

CLIFF: Oh yes. Here he is. Good God, do you see how old he is?

J.P.: No.

CLIFF: Forty-one.

J.P.: They're getting like the policemen.

CLIFF: What's *he* on about?

J.P.: The newly created Bishop of Bromley, the Right Rev. Ted Sprogg, yesterday lashed out at the backward elements in his diocese. Sitting in his newly opened cafeteria in the Cathedral Close, the Reverend Ted, seen here with his wife Meryl, who will refuse to wear the outmoded mitre and ecclesiastical gear at his enthronement next month, was wearing jeans and an open-necked shirt, as he spelled out the future in today's plain terms. The new bishop, author of the controversial *An Unemployed Teenager Speaks with Christ*, author also of *Christ, the Good European* and *Those Feet in Europe's Green and Pleasant Land*, told his enthusiastic assembled flock what they could expect.

CLIFF: I got quite fond of Mark One.

J.P.: Gone with the perils of this night, that comfort which the

20

world cannot give and that service which is perfect freedom.

(*Church bells start ringing.* CLIFF *puts down paper to listen.* ALISON *can't hear them.* J.P. *gets up slowly, goes to the window, looks out, then opens it. They are immediately much louder. He listens.*)

CLIFF: Bloody bells . . . Why don't you close the bloody window?

J.P.: I like to *hear* them . . . (*Pauses at the ironing board.*) Ring in the larger heart . . . the kindlier hand . . . Ring out the darkness of the land.

CLIFF: Don't they know someone's going mad in here? That poor girl's in a draught.

(J.P. *sits.*)

J.P.: Endless changes can be rung.

CLIFF: Can't hear.

J.P.: On church bells of the English tongue. You know we sometimes said . . .

CLIFF: What?

J.P.: Said all our children would be Americans.

CLIFF: You may have done. I never went in for that kind of grandiloquent small talk.

J.P.: Pity about America. If only it had grown up. I was very fond of it.

CLIFF: They were very nice to you.

J.P.: Now it's the Australian Age. Antipodea or the Recidivists' Revenge.

CLIFF: Well, I suppose the lower middle classes had their kingdom coming to them. A three-piece suite is the same the world over, right way up or upside down.

J.P.: How wise you are, in your simple open-hearted way, mighty continent, strainful strine, dark and unlovely suburb of the loveless desert . . .

CLIFF: Kookaburras flying duck-like on our every wall.

J.P.: Enthusiasm not appreciated. Effete and Pommie. You can't *impress* an Aussie however you squeeze their sun-baked leathery hearts. O Lord, let me not be lower middle class.

CLIFF: Well – keep trying.

J.P.: Above all, protect me from the Australian Hun.

CLIFF: Do you think God is an Australian?

J.P.: Most certainly. *And* a woman. Ah, there he is His
Grace, the Right Rev. Ted Bromley, himself a native of
New Zealand, from Auckland, in fact, which, if you
rate Sydney as the Byzantium *de nos jours* on your cultural
Richter scale, is somewhere between the twin dioceses of
Canberra and Milton Keynes. An interloper to his horny
fingertips, he speaks with the tongue of the horrible Brit,
a brutal breed he has helped create in the wake of his
seething, colonial act of revenge. Why, your craven
ursine friend there would give his best furry pair of
fourteen-hole Doc Martens to find the favours of koalas like
Noylene, Norene, Charlene and Chlorine, all ripped timely
from that knuckle of abandonment and unease, old
Ockers rib, chundered up in seven strife-borne days, the
flattest, most barren place and disappointment's most
isolated and lonely land, to fret and squabble beneath the
unforgiving sun and surf. If we'd had (*Australian accent*) as
many Abos as the Boers had Kaffirs, we'd have wiped 'em
out with a few well-aimed tubes of Myne. I tell you the
day will shortly come – and it's difficult to sustain this
mangled speech in northern climes – when a man may
move from the Tigris to the Euphrates, from the Thames,
the Seine, the Danube and the Rhine, even to the Nile, and
proclaim, like wandering scholars of a thousand years, *vis
Australius ad sum* and go unmolested, revered and
understood.

CLIFF: He does exaggerate, don't you, whitey? Still, he's
happy . . .

J.P.: Did you ever miss the old sweet stall?

CLIFF: No.

J.P.: Neither did I.

CLIFF: It was better than working.

J.P.: Her boyfriend, young Anfony. Now he's a born
Australian.

CLIFF: Anfony?

J.P.: So, come to that, are your two likewise recidivist sons, the beasts of Bedales.

CLIFF: Bedales was Ellie's fault.

J.P.: You gave in to her uppity notions of academic chic. Rubbing shoulders with all those lighting cameramen, chairpersons and furniture designers, being abandoned to rely on their own minuscule imaginations, so painfully reading the instructions on a condom packet and getting it wrong. Shall I tell you an Australian joke?

CLIFF: No.

J.P.: Non-racist?

CLIFF: Later.

J.P.: A joke based, naturally, upon stereotypes. That is to say, the common-sense ordinary, observation.

CLIFF: Alison's feeling a bit frail.

J.P.: Why? She's been asleep ever since she came down here. About eighteen hours.

CLIFF: She's tired –

J.P.: We're all tired. She doesn't have to bring all that bloody ironing with her, does she? I shall burn that ironing board. *I've* never used it. It's a *plot* . . . Teddy's very quiet.

CLIFF: Thinking, I expect.

J.P.: Oh?

CLIFF: He looks thoughtful.

ALISON: Maybe he's bored.

J.P.: Oh, you *can* hear.

CLIFF: He's too polite. And caring.

J.P.: If he's bored he can get up and go. Whenever.

CLIFF: Oh, he still enjoys a joke. Just like the next bear.

J.P.: But not Teddyist jokes?

CLIFF: He's very vulnerable.

J.P.: Aren't we all? Thin-skinned, I think you mean. Like all dissemblers, he shrinks from hard words. Thinks he's cuddlesome, I suppose.

CLIFF: He is.

J.P.: So are lioncubs. But they like raw meat.

CLIFF: Teddy's aware that to survive he must become increasingly competitive.

J.P.: So he should.

ALISON: I thought bears were –

   (J.P. *looks up sharply*.)

J.P.: What?

ALISON: Oh – Beautiful?

J.P.: Not the way you say it.

CLIFF: Bears *is* beautiful. Was.

J.P.: Bears is often bullies.

CLIFF: So might you be if you were a persecuted minority.

J.P.: You mean rancorous and noisy?

CLIFF: Ah, colonel, you've no feelings.

J.P.: I have, but I don't present them as cuddlesome.

ALISON: Not in your case they aren't.

CLIFF: She's right there.

J.P.: Some have found me passing cuddlesome.

CLIFF: Who?

J.P.: Anyway, he's not half as cuddlesome as he's made out.

CLIFF: There! You *do* resent him.

J.P.: I don't.

CLIFF: Yes, you do. You only see him as a stereotype.

J.P.: Isn't he? Believe me, I often don't think about him at all.

CLIFF: You mean you don't care what happens to him?

J.P.: Being vulnerable at his age is boring. It should be overcome.

CLIFF: He never had a role model.

J.P.: Neither did I. Even fallen sparrows learnt to fly once.

CLIFF: No one gave him wings.

J.P.: Tell him to grow some.

CLIFF: He hates your loathsome materialism. He really does.

J.P.: So do I.

CLIFF: It's sickening to contemplate the way this country treats its Teddies.

J.P.: The ones who cry over Teddy never lived next to him.

CLIFF: This constant sanctification of greed.

J.P.: You bet – all I think about is where my next hot buttered toast is coming from.

CLIFF: Teddy doesn't believe he's truly boring.

24

J.P.: Only the truly mad believe they're sane. I'd say that bear could do with a spoonful of reticence in his morning honey.

CLIFF: You've never suffered the marginalization of being a bear. The harassment, the prejudice.

J.P.: Yes, I have. It's on the record.

CLIFF: Never unemployed.

J.P.: *I* got myself a sweet stall, remember, dreamboat?

CLIFF: *You* never grew up with an outside toilet.

J.P.: The cold wind round a young bear's parts doesn't seem the worst wound life can inflict. Besides, if he'd troubled to read the neatly cut-up newspapers hung handily and ingeniously on the empty toilet roll, he might have overcome his snivelling illiteracy.

CLIFF: All right for you. *You* live in a big house.

J.P.: Yes, but I keep two rooms in a Sunderland back-to-back just so I don't lose contact with my working-class roots – and where I can give interviews to the press.

CLIFF: Teddy is going to take his case to the European Court of Human Rights.

J.P.: Teddy – is not, I'm sorry – human.

CLIFF: Oh yes? How do you *know*?

J.P.: I don't.

CLIFF: Exactly . . .

J.P.: How right you are.

CLIFF: I'm afraid so.

J.P.: It's taken me almost, well, indeed, a lifetime to realize that I am wrong about – well, everything.

CLIFF: About time, my dear friend. About time.

J.P.: Yes. None too soon.

CLIFF: No wonder he's gone quiet.

J.P.: There should be a Sunday moratorium on Teddy's big mouth.

ALISON: Say that again.

J.P.: I wish he'd shift his comfortable big arse down to the cellar for me.

CLIFF: *He* doesn't want an alcohol problem.

J.P.: To him, anything pleasurable's a problem.

CLIFF: The trouble is –

J.P.: Make him shut up.

ALISON: Please, Cliff.

(*They both look at him.*)

CLIFF: He's asked me to tell you –

J.P.: Well?

CLIFF: He wants to get out of all this and –

J.P.: What?

CLIFF: Start living in the real world of today.

J.P.: Does he? He always did have a whimsical streak.

(J.P. *returns to his paper.* CLIFF *going on when the game is closed* . . .)

CLIFF: I suppose you were going to say if he doesn't like it here he can always go back to where he first came from.

J.P.: Precisely. A list of caring agencies is kept on the dresser where even he can reach it. You too. In the china-squirrel bank. Any time. Go back to sleep. Damn!

CLIFF: What is it?

J.P.: I've lost the Bishop of Bromley. Have you got him?

CLIFF: No. Don't think so.

J.P.: You *must* have. (*Pause.*) You know what's wrong?

CLIFF: Tell us, anyway.

J.P.: These. (*Holds up a quality Sunday paper.*) When we couldn't afford them, we spun them out the whole Sabbath. Look at that: a week's deadweight of investigative insight – interviewing junk. Why are you so *slow*, Porter. Once you could waste your energies for a passing laugh. You could take on the excesses of tedium, but no longer. You haven't the time. Look to your trusty filleting knife. (*Begins deftly to 'fillet' the papers.*) Business section: certainly not. Sport: banished from this house at all times. New Society: can damage your health. Appointments: no interest whatever. (*He applies himself to the rest beside Teddy.*)

CLIFF: Hey, not the sport.

J.P.: Out, damned sport. Review of the Week. All of you. (*Regards the* New Statesman.) Surely no one reads *that* any more.

CLIFF: Not the supplements.

J.P.: You used to do very well without them. Be brave. You don't want to know about some smug's room of his/her own or favourite Sunday.

CLIFF: Well, it's not this.

J.P.: There. (*Shoulders a pile of papers and magazines.*) Out! All of you. (*Takes them to the window and throws them out.*) There! That's better! You'll feel the benefit of it, later!

CLIFF: Bit drastic, if you ask me.

J.P.: Monday morning will be all the better for you. (*Pause.*) Oh, how I long for a little warm, inhuman reticence.

CLIFF: What?

J.P.: I do. For modesty and men and persons not twitching with opinions, they are flea-ridden with grievance for others, all honking behind you. I wish to remain in the slow lane, thank you. I *am* slow, reticent, modest. Dated but still powerful.
(*Sings:*)
> Teddy'll work for de local guvmin,
> Teddies all work for de town hall boss,
> Tings dat make de anti-racist cross.
> Don't look up man!
> Don't look down.
> You don't dass made de black boss frown . . .

It's started to rain.

CLIFF: Wouldn't you know . . .

J.P.: Are you going to talk like that for the rest of your life? Did you know it was National – or is it International – Motivation Year? Or was it Week? How did you know?

CLIFF: I told you.

J.P.: When?

CLIFF: I don't know. (*To* ALISON) Didn't I?

J.P.: Have you met the boyfriend, Anfony? Yes. Yes, you have. *He's* in search of motivation. Very short of it. Offer him the smallest handy grappling iron up the mountain slope and his reply? (*Yob accent*) '*Well*, it's not wurf my while, is it?' Anfony's whiles are almost beyond price or ingenuity . . . Not unlike those little sonny Jims of yours and, before it goes unsaid, mine own poor thing. Ah, but they like

27

expensive things to slurp with their beefburgers, beans and chips. The only time those brooding lads ever acknowledge me at all when you bring them to my house for a little easeful conviviality is when I rattle the stick in the champagne bucket. Over they lope, hop skip and grunt, their knuckles brushing the floor. What does that elder son of yours want to be when he grows up?

CLIFF: An adolescent.

J.P.: Ah, like his grandparents.

CLIFF: He's not so bad.

J.P.: No?

CLIFF: He just wants to believe in something.

J.P.: How admirable. Like my own young feller-me-lad.

CLIFF: I don't know about my lot but young Jimmy's up against a lot of things that weren't around for us.

J.P.: You mean you and I were more fortunate?

CLIFF: Looks like it.

J.P.: The old sweet stall was a lucky break?

CLIFF: You're pretending not to understand.

J.P.: Oh, I think I understand. I don't think your lads – or mine – would have been so fanciful.

CLIFF: I thought you said you'd enjoyed it.

J.P.: It was what I believe young actresses call 'a challenge'.

CLIFF: They don't seem to be offered much hope.

J.P.: Hope comes from within, as you well know, my poor old guilty goosey. Be proud. You have thrived, by virtue of your modest talents, in a cold and poisonous world. When hope goes, we freeze. No, they are not chilled, not with despair, why should they be? Maybe it will come but not now. There is too much noise, comfort and distraction. For the likes of young Jimmy. How I hate diminutives. My real friends stopped calling me Jimmy long ago. Oh . . . I suppose more or less when Alison left me. (*He regards his daughter broodingly*.) She doesn't have to do that, you know.

CLIFF: What's that, honky?

J.P.: All that bloody ironing. She's dressed like a long-haul truck driver since she was twelve and yet, whenever she's

28

here, she's perched up there like the young brides of my childhood, smoothing away at the silks and embroidered crêpe de Chine of their trousseaus to be lovingly laid to rest among their layers of whispering tissue paper in the bottom drawer. It can't be for Anfony. Ironing a man's shirt, even as an act of absent-minded kindliness, would be a blasphemy against her sisterhood. Perhaps it's for her old chum and blood-sister Helena. (*To* ALISON) Has she taken to dressing up as Mrs Danvers then? Your friend? Ms Helena? She would look somewhat fetching in bombazine and leg-of-mutton sleeves. That and a stout bunch of keys. Have you noticed how portly the miners have become? Like the bishops getting younger. You must have noticed, Alison.

(ALISON *lifts her Walkman headset, frowning.*)

ALISON: What's that?

J.P.: You were in on all those appeals with colliers' wives when they were flipping concrete blocks like tiddly-winks on the heads of passing cab-drivers, scabbing lackeys of the greedy classes. Raising money for the kiddies' Christmas toys as I remember, wasn't it? Did you notice how your average collier had grown a little obese? And why not?

(ALISON *returns to her headphones.*)

Those stringy whippet creatures in the tin bath before the kitchen hob, all blue-black coal, pocked backs and ribcages, those hard, forbearing men, steel stretched, merciless fatigue, them and their back-scrubbing, wholesome women, all gone with their scrubbed front steps, all gone, good and quite right. How do you suppose old Lawrence D. H. would have borne down over the kiddies' poor little faces as they faced Christmas without their hi-tech toys and the two extra weeks in the Costa gone?

(ALISON *looks at him, turns to the window and looks at the billowing newspapers. We see the reverse of her T-shirt, on which is written:* J.P. RULES, OK.

J.P. *goes over to the ironing board. He and* ALISON *begin a ritual game of staring each other out. Whatever childhood habit and affection there may have once been in this is quickly dissipated. They resume their customary, mutual, baleful boredom.)*

J.P.: *(Quietly, thrusting magazine at her)* Do you know who that is?

ALISON: *(Barely glancing)* Yeah.

J.P.: You do!

ALISON: Umm.

J.P.: And her? What about her?

ALISON: Yeah.

J.P.: You mean – you really do know who they are?

ALISON: So?

J.P.: Both?

ALISON: Are you kidding? No, you're not.

J.P.: Good God . . . *(To CLIFF)* You don't know who they are? Well, do you?

CLIFF: Just about. *(Looking)* Yes. Well, I do have children of that age.

J.P.: So do I . . . Remember Brother Nigel?

CLIFF: Not really.

J.P.: Ah, the rewards of wordmanship. Well, Brother Nigel had a bit of a turtley old voice in the land when you and I were quite indifferent to bettering ourselves, getting on or making some meaning of our lives. Old Nigel was at it, doing all of these things. Back bencher, loyalty, late knighthood, mind you. Alison's dad finally left him some hundred and fifty thousand quid. London railways, Penang rubber. All helped with the house in Godalming and the fees for Marlborough. Any road, *(newspaper)* here's young Brother Nigel the second. Guess what he's become? An MEP no less. Minister for European pricks. MEP. Or Most Empty Person. Author of *Everything YOU Ever Wanted to Know About Europe*. He delights in full-time wrangling over the permitted length of bananas and the permissible centimetres demanded for the comfort of imported tortoises. From Brother Nigel of Outer Space to the United States of Civilization and all the beckoning goodies of the yes, twenty-first century. I said to the man at the gate of

the century. Open up. Let us in. And there's young Nigel
Junior waiting to let us in. When I remember how I used
to make light of his father in my youthful cheap wont, I see
the present paucity of my own motivation, my
inapprehension of the future. Here is young Nigel,
Motivational European Person, leading the way with a
three-column photograph in the undiscarded Business
Section. Young Nigel. 1992 . . . You know where I went
wrong?

CLIFF: You haven't really chucked the sports section?

J.P.: You don't want me to be a passive victim of your Sunday
section abuse, do you? I did think, I suppose, that those
with what you might call privilege, the inheritance of
confidence, family, shares, partnerships and heirlooms, a
small regency card table that comes your way, a friendly
cousin in the law or army, an uncle housemaster
somewhere, being put up for your father's club, bygone
perks, I thought these little gifts distributed unjustly to the
likes of Brother Nigel rendered him unteachable. But I was
wrong. No, it was the people I'd thought of as being
oppressed or ignored by Nigel or Alison, Nigel and Alison,
who were unteachable. They were avid and malign. Like
those Ministry of Food women who used to preside over
their trestle tables in provincial town halls, allocating ration
books, if they felt like it, puffed up with power and
illiteracy. They felt so secure behind their trestle barricades
and ministerial stamps. 'You'll have to fill in Form NF72.
Why haven't you got one?' They were the post-war sappers
for all the rolling army of fanatics that have followed them
ever since. I don't think we used to know many fanatics,
did we?

CLIFF: The Builders Arms was pretty famous.

J.P.: I don't mean lunatics. I mean fanatics. The lady from the
department with her briefcase at your door, the one that
came the other week, the one with, yes, statutory powers.
Lunatics do not have statutory powers.

ALISON: Did your wife get any of it?

J.P.: (*Surprised*) What?

ALISON: Her father's money?

J.P.: The middle classes never tell you when they've made a killing, especially when it's inherited money. I imagine Brother Nigel saw she was all right, as he saw it – he having the responsibilities, wife and three kids to educate. Alison looked very sparkling to me last time I saw her – that place San Antonio's with a pack of nancy friends hot from some runaway gala for Aids Concern. I don't think old Mummy would have been too happy to see her fawned on by so many strutting sodomites in a public place. The old rhino might have roared a bit at that.

ALISON: I went to that gala. It was very special and moving.

J.P.: I hope so. I really do.

ALISON: She read wonderfully. She really did.

J.P.: Good.

ALISON: Why don't you just shut up?

CLIFF: Yes. You know nothing about it.

J.P.: Of course I don't. How could I abandon my habitual diffidence, that diffidence of all right-thinking men?

CLIFF: You're pissed, J.P.

J.P.: What were we talking about before I blundered off? Oh, ah –

ALISON: The Australian Age, the Edwardian Age.

J.P.: Well, not much to say about that. Oh yes, except that it never existed. The *on dit* is that there never were long days in the sun, the slim volumes of verse. If the linen was crisp, some laundry maid's cracked hands had paid the price for it. As for the smell of starch, it was quite possibly poisonous and nothing so special. No, not only did we, did I at least, footlingly regret the passing of other people's worlds, they were ones we'd just confected for our vulgar comfort.

(*While* J.P.'s *saying this, he fiddles with a tape recorder and then sings a song of almost sublime banality, 'In a Little Gypsy Tea Room'. It is a ballad of the period of his childhood: the thirties; sung most famously by Arthur Tracey, 'The Street Singer'. However, the daunting task for the actor is to sing this with an unmocking sweetness so that it may almost overcome the*

32

*cloying nonsense of the ballad itself. For most, it will hurtle
the spectator into cool embarrassment – like* ALISON.
*Certainly a kamikaze test of the potency of cheap music. The
tape accompaniment should ideally consist of a piano
accordion.*)

I was seeking shelter from the weather,
It was on a rainy April day.
You remember how we got together,
In a shop across the way.
After being caught with my umbrella,
I stepped in to have a cup of tea,
Just for fun I called the fortune-teller,
What a lucky day for me.
It was in a little gypsy tea room,
When I was feelin' blue.
It was in a little gypsy tea room,
I first laid eyes on you.
When the gypsy came to read the tealeaves,
It made me feel quite gay,
When she said that someone in the tea room,
Would steal my heart away.
Right there in front of my eyes.
With the smell that's sweeter than the roses,
You made a dream come true.
It was in a little gypsy tea room,
I gave my heart to you.
I really thought it unremarkable,
But just imagine my surprise,
She made the story quite believable,
Right there in front of my eyes.
With a smile that's sweeter than the roses,
You made a dream come true.
It was in a little gypsy tea room,
I gave my heart to you.

(*Pause.*)

Strange how impotent cheap music is. Do you suppose
there ever was such a thing as a gypsy tea room?

CLIFF: Never know . . .

J.P.: I can see the girl in it. I can certainly see myself. (*Sings:*) 'You made a dream come true.'

CLIFF: 'It made me feel quite gay.' Pretty poor tea, I should think.

J.P.: Oh, I don't know. Hot buttered toast, oozing with cholesterol. Some dainty cakes. Of course, the Gypsy Tea Room, if it existed, which it didn't, wasn't Edwardian, so it wouldn't have been too robust, even in the imagination. I think I'd have been a small boy in the corner, watching the man and the girl come in from the rain, thinking of myself as him.

CLIFF: Sounds a bit like a Kelvinside tea shop I went into one morning for a baptie. Slower than McDonald's but more romantic.

J.P.: Camp, you'd say?

CLIFF: McDonald's is scarcely camp. Just bright and beastly. Sorry, Alison.

ALISON: For what?

CLIFF: Can you hear with all that pounding in your ears?

ALISON: I've listened to him talking all my life. No group could entirely drown that.

(J.P. *gently removes the earphones from her head and puts them on his own.*)

J.P.: What pretty ears, pink, pearly lobes. How I do remember them between the tips of my fingers. (*Listens.*) Something strong, something simple, something. Something English. (*He puts the set back on her head and goes over to a large portable record player, turns it on. An immediate blast of rock 'n' roll sounds shakes the room. He has to shout to make himself heard.*)

Are you going to your concert, your gig, tonight? With Anfony. Are you going to *wave*? Have you noticed, Mildred, how they wave, like fields of rape, have you watched, they sway, like multitudinous stalks, they wave, limp and twitching like bleary puppies. Watch me, wave, wave and sway, come, Whittaker, wave and sway. O wave new world, proud and sound, brave, young, fearless, numb and gormless, they wave, side to side, arms stretched up, worshipping, side to side, fixed on the choreographic grunt, so tangible in the fullness of its torpor. Nuremberg was never so fine, so fluent. They are young, their hard baby fists softly flailing at the air, remote, in their thrumping, plaintive battering unison, boning fields, landscapes of them, a prairie of Babel, waving and smashing, waving, fingers fluttering, beating, supplicant wings to what we know not, wave, sway stare gaze, wave, wave . . . deafening, submerging, deadly, sea plants limp and poisonous, wading . . .

(During all this he mimes the waving gestures of massed pop concerts, encouraging CLIFF, *achieving what should be quite an inventive piece of fairly artful mockery. When all this has gone on long enough,* ALISON *picks up the ironing board and throws it at him. Pause. The ironing board has caught him a hefty blow and his hand goes up to his head. He stands, swaying slightly. Presently, and in a quiet confidential tone of relief, he speaks.)*

You know, I was always hoping that my first wife would do that. She never did. I would see people urging her on with their eyes, shrieking silently from within: 'Chuck the bloody ironing board at him.' She was too strong, too fortified, certainly against anything as inconsequential to her as myself, too wily and wised-up to press any red buttons.

ALISON: Who do you think you bloody are?

J.P.: No one of any interest whatever.

ALISON: I think you're mad and utterly horrible.

J.P.: I don't know why you ever come back here. I've nothing to offer you.

ALISON: You bet. You've never had anything to offer *anyone*.

J.P.: Candour suits you. You should draw on it more often.

ALISON: I come to see my brother, not you.

J.P.: I think you'll find him hemmed in by supporters. Your friend, the Rev. Ron, at the head of them. Vandals are a protected species in the Church.

ALISON: Why did you ever marry that poor woman? Or my mother, for that matter?

J.P.: It did legitimize you. It seemed proper at the time.

ALISON: Don't be so fucking cheap. Why bother to *have* us?

J.P.: Not to perpetuate myself, I assure you.

ALISON: That's something anyway. And, thank God, you haven't.

J.P.: That's a lot of questions. I'm sure you don't want me to attempt to answer them.

ALISON: No fear.

(ALISON *starts collecting up her clothes, readjusting her Walkman and cutting herself off from any further contact.*)

J.P.: (*To* CLIFF) My old dog's dying you know.

CLIFF: I didn't know.

J.P.: Well, I didn't want to spread gloom and despondency. I sat with her all last night and this morning. I'd better go again.

ALISON: (*As he is about to pass her*) Go on. Talk to your bloody dog. She can't answer back.

(ALISON *fixes her earphones firmly back in place and 'waves' in mockery of* J.P.'*s earlier parody.*)

J.P.: Are you angry?

ALISON: What do you think?

J.P.: (*Softly*) I think not. Anger is not hatred, which is what I see in all your faces. Anger is slow, gentle, not vindictive or full of spite. Also, it comes into the world in grief not grievance.

ALISON: Couldn't hear you, old cock. Nobody wants to hear *you*!

(ALISON '*waves*', *dancing to the sound in her ears. Coherence has begun to desert* J.P., *but he struggles to retain it.*)

J.P.: (*Still softly*) 'What's he angry *about*?' they used to ask. Anger is not *about* . . . It is mourning the unknown, the loss of what went before without you, it's the love another time but not this might have sprung on you, and greatest loss of all, the deprivation of what, even as a child, seemed to be irrevocably your own, your country, your birthplace, that, at least, is as tangible as death.

(ALISON '*waves*' *defiantly. Deliberately,* J.P. *removes her*

36

headphones, picks up the attached instrument, drops it to the
floor and steps on it. It crackles and breaks.)

ALISON: (*Presently*) Oh – well done, J.P.

J.P.: I do try not to behave like the people I most despise.

ALISON: You're pathetic . . .

J.P.: No doubt. But *I* shall rally. *You* will never grapple with
defeat. I refuse to allow a noisome prig in jeans and no bra
to make me lose my good humour for no good reason.

CLIFF: Noisome's a good word.

J.P.: I am not known as El Cheapo for nothing.

(*He goes to the door.*)

    The name is Porter,
    My critics curse on.
    I am a better class of person,
    Mangy of fur; at no time chic,
    I dine in hellfire twice a week.

(*He goes out.*)

ALISON: 'El Cheapo' is right . . .

CLIFF: Well – Teddy liked it . . .

ACT TWO

SCENE I

The same. CLIFF *is seated.* ALISON *stares out of the window.*
Pause.

CLIFF: Teddy's quiet . . . I think he's given up brooding over
market forces. Just concentrating on trying to become a
good European. He's been hanging back for too long from
playing a full role in unification, haven't you? Starting a
new fast-lane lifestyle aren't you, my old ursine cocky?
Even feeling a little less guilty over his colonial past. Aren't
you? Less guilty? His part in the slave trade, for instance.
About a hundred and fifty years before his time but it
bothers him. Wouldn't think he had a colonial past to look
at him, would you? Well, that's his considered view of it.
Isn't it?
(CLIFF *gropes among the newspapers for a black, hairy object*
which turns out to be a dreadlock wig. He arranges it on
Teddy's head.)
That degree course in African Studies and Caribbean
Culture didn't cheer him up either. He will worry about
people, especially if he doesn't know them. Don't you,
Ted? You *worry* . . . That wig's a mistake. Do you think he
secretly hates whitey?
ALISON: Teddy – can go fuck himself.
CLIFF: He already thinks he's in a no-win situation.
ALISON: You know what? You two are mad. Barking.
CLIFF: Teddy's not mad. Not he that is gone into England.
ALISON: Oh, do *shut* up, Cliff. When he's not here, *you* start to
sound like my father.
CLIFF: Perhaps a little mad but no, not malign. Ted never had a
role model, you see. Not even a world that never existed to
regret.
ALISON: You've both talked this brand of babyish balls ever
since I can remember.
CLIFF: You wrong-footed him pretty adroitly just now.

38

ALISON: Oh? I goaded him, *I* exposed the vicious oik struggling inside every carping old dodo like J.P. Longing for some petty recompense for a lifetime of useless snarling. No wonder he prefers dogs to people. He came into this world bitching and he'll go out the same way. Unloved, unlovable and unloving.

CLIFF: Teddy's quite fond of him.

ALISON: Then Teddy *is* mad. *And* malign.

CLIFF: Did you never like him ever? As a little girl? At all?

ALISON: No.

CLIFF: Well – you didn't see much of each other. Your mother saw to that.

ALISON: She wanted to protect me.

CLIFF: Against what?

ALISON: Someone so rabid hopeless. With such a second, third-rate, oh, mind.

CLIFF: Well, your mother has an obsession with what her sort of friends call 'first-class minds'. I don't think J.P.'s second class. What British Rail call 'Standard' perhaps. J.P., a most happily prejudiced witness, tells me that your mother's old love, Professor Randy, First Class Brain, was devastated when his wife died before Christmas. The reason being that he no longer had the perfect hostess for his dinners in London when he popped up from Oxford for his weekend performances. More seriously, he found at an advancing age, and to his great astonishment, that he could no longer get it up. He's been inconsolable for weeks. Even your mother's attentions with mid-morning smoked salmon and her best Wine Society claret in the evenings haven't brought him comfort.

ALISON: There's nothing wrong in being brainy.

CLIFF: I met a girl once. In Cannes. I was sitting on the terrace, having breakfast and reading *The Times*. She was sitting at the next table, looking quite gorgeous at that time of day. Suddenly, she looked up and said, rather coldly I thought: 'What have you got for seventeen down?' Seventeen what? 'The crossword. You've got it there.' Oh, I thought: There goes that one. 'I'm sorry: I don't do *The Times* crossword.'

Her beautiful lip curled, it really did. 'You don't? And how do you exercise your mind?' No joy there, I thought. Exercise my mind? By fucking intellectual girls like you.

ALISON: Why do you try so hard to be unpleasant? There's nothing wrong in being brainy. She admires intellect. So what? So do I.

CLIFF: There's such a thing as decent intellect. Like dumb insolence.

ALISON: She's accustomed to the company of clever men. She comes from a clever family. Her parents, her brothers.

CLIFF: Ah yes, barristers, judges.

ALISON: Yes, all right: diplomats, scholars, historians.

CLIFF: And the cleverness of strangers too. Not an MEP among them. You wouldn't call J.P.'s family clever. More silly to themselves, eh, Ted? You must have your mother's intellect.

ALISON: (*Fierce*) What's he ever given me – forget *done* for me? And *don't* say 'What's he ever done for Teddy?' Sometimes I think you're worse than he is. At least he seems to *enjoy* being a bully and a bigot – every now and then.

CLIFF: J.P.? He's just an old dog. Now, I'd say your mother's a bully.

ALISON: She isn't.

CLIFF: She sends you up here to report on him.

ALISON: Is that what he says?

CLIFF: Why else would you come up here so regularly? When you despise him.

ALISON: Oh, and you think young Jimmy comes up to spy as well?

CLIFF: I think your brother's too unconcerned to hitchhike two hundred miles to eavesdrop on his father. He comes up for free meals, twenty-four-hour sleeps, a hefty tip and, possibly, even some respite from your mummy. Dad's place is an all-right squat, and, if there's a great gig up the road in the big city, OK.

ALISON: You must think we're hard up.

CLIFF: You forget. I have children of my own.

ALISON: Well, he's sure not doing much about his son being jumped on by the police.

CLIFF: He's talked about nothing else since *I* came up.

ALISON: Oh yes. Jimmy may go to prison. And where's his father? Slumped over a filthy old blanket in his posh drawing room we're not allowed in, keening like a peasant over a cheesy old dog.

CLIFF: I think young Jimmy is happier where he is – with the Rev. Ron. Anyway, the dog does love him.

ALISON: Yeah. Like Teddy, I suppose.

CLIFF: I don't think he is quite sure. 'Occasionally held but never moved,' as they say. I've learned very little during the time I've seen you grow up, but one small thing has become clear to me, that, apart from the fact of realizing that one's parents may be corrupt or even wicked, your children may also be vindictive and even vengeful. Above all, as with your ironing-board pantomime, something stares you in the early-morning face: that those whom you no longer love can still inflict amazing pain.

ALISON: On *him*? Who?

CLIFF: Yourself. Your mother, young Jimmy even.

ALISON: He's never loved anyone. Not even himself and God knows that *does* make sense.

CLIFF: Forgive me, Alison. I *was* there. You weren't. I really do think you feel oppressed as you say you are because you had a man for a father.

ALISON: Oh, very J. Porter. Most glib. I'd get on the first train to Euston in the morning if I were you. Go back to your wife, even your children, go back to the TV studios, go back to Wales, even. Teddy and J.P. will only bring you down to their own silly level.

CLIFF: I don't come back to spy on him.

ALISON: Do you think my mother cares what happens to him? J. Porter Esquire? He doesn't exist. For any of us.

CLIFF: Perhaps he never did. It's the one thing you might have all agreed about.

ALISON: Don't be so bloody precious.

CLIFF: You're right. Maybe it's these bloody church bells. I always told him it was a mistake having a church tower next door to your runner beans. It was bad enough in the old days, when they made him angry. I dare say the Rev. Ron will silence all that with a strong rock beat soon enough. What message do they have for young people today? Decadence, shabby sentiment, yes, what J.P. calls 'the crimson twilight'. Those were our Sunday evenings. Bloody bells. Unheeded, élitist bells. But then I was brought up a Methodist. Leave him alone, Alison.

ALISON: With pleasure.

CLIFF: He may not have lightened up your life but he hasn't darkened it.

ALISON: And he won't. Don't you think you can drop all this seedy male conspiracy for a bit? What's he going to do for his own son when he's in such trouble? That's what I've come to find out.

CLIFF: Nothing. I imagine.

ALISON: There you are.

CLIFF: Your mother didn't exactly hurtle back from her US lecture tour. Just a few gushy phone calls and a list of pushy lawyers who only appear for the grievously oppressed.

ALISON: That tour is important to her career.

CLIFF: Quite so. That's a consideration J.P. hasn't got. Still, the Rev. Ron's barged to the front like a funeral parlour executive at a pile-up on the motorway.

(*Telephone rings offstage.* ALISON *and* CLIFF *both wait to see if it's answered. It stops.* CLIFF *grabs the local paper and reads:*)

'James Hugh Porter, aged twenty, of 17 Burne-Jones Villas, W11, pleaded not guilty to seven charges of arson and malicious damage to church property.' There must be church property nearer home, around Burne-Jones Villas? Why did he come all the way up here for a spot of the Saturday Night Vandals? Blah, blah. 'Porter's parents were not in court.' Here we are. 'The Rev. Ron Peplow, who stood bail for the two youths, one of them his own son,

Anthony, said outside the court, "Our society is looking for scapegoats for its spiritual and political failure." '

(*Enter* J.P. *He is carrying a Walkman-style machine.*)

' "This unhappy incident may spotlight and target in" ' – there's a telling phrase from a man of God – ' "target in on the complacent and uncaring forces that have produced our inner cities and their tragedy may now be about to be visited upon our more comfortable and enclosed little world." '

J.P.: These words, these disturbing incidents, prompt us to ask: 'How long have we been living in an unreal world?'

CLIFF: Or the world in real terms.

ALISON: Here we go.

(J.P. *hands her the Walkman.*)

J.P.: There. I was keeping one in reserve. In case of contingencies.

(ALISON *takes it and sets it down.*)

No, the Rev. Ron targeted in pretty smartly but our own editor sounded a rallying cry to the nation.

(*He takes the paper from* CLIFF.)

Where are we? 'The New Model Army Invades the Heart of England.' Young Jimmy – one of Cromwell's men.

(*Reads, quick and smarmy:*) 'We are used to reading of mindless violence in our inner cities but this week we find it exploding right here on our own doorstep, the heartland of England. Here, secure as we thought from the blight of post-industrial despair, we find ourselves invaded by a new model army intent on what must appear to us to be unmotivated reprisal on an innocent, law-abiding community, proud of its ancient heritage and still trying to uphold and honour its spiritual endowment. Blah, blah. Where its tiny town hall still displays its Latin charter of 1573 proclaiming freedom from the tyranny of troops and even princes. An act of barbarism has been perpetrated in our midst which makes us shudder for the future. We will only add that the two young men who face these allegations are both from comfortable middle-class homes. They have, thank God, the right to a full and fair trial. We say only

43

this: that this was an outrage committed by persons as yet unknown, not in the new purpose-built cities of the twenty-first century but in the kind of small and ancient towns we assumed were still outposts against the vandalism of modern urban life.'

CLIFF: The Inner City. It sounds like the Bishop of Bromley's hard-hitting best-seller on spiritual agony.

J.P.: That's why his spokespersons like old Rev. Ron invented it. They wouldn't know an inner city if it was dropped on their heads like a collier's tiddly-wink. Detroit, *there's* an inner city for you, damnable and desolate within. Los Angeles, the cities of the plains, the Midwest, hemmed in by the moonface of America, the desert heart of it. Outside the city you come to its limits, there's just the great swathe of highway America ahead; you leave the checkpoint, abandoned to those spaces that erode history and defy memorial. There is nowhere to go under the world-weight of that sky, no place to shelter from the enormity of that primal intolerance. No, their cities were not like our chokey towns nobbut more than a tram ride from those hills of ancient time, not so old that they can't seem like your very own memory, a homely antiquity, obedient and comforting. You can have a snooze in a hedge and listen to the chesty cough of the skylark or lean on the top of the moor but you don't take a stroll in the prairie. That's why the Americans never go for a walk. There's nowhere – on the way.

CLIFF: I think the last tram left Leeds about 1960.

J.P.: Oh? I didn't notice. (*To* ALISON) That was your friend Helena. She's visiting Jimmy at the Rev. Ron's. But the place seems to be full up. I said she could stay here.

ALISON: (*Astonished*) Did you?

J.P.: *She* seemed surprised.

ALISON: Your last meeting wasn't very pleasant.

J.P.: Oh, I think she enjoyed taking a few sisterly bites out of my ankle. Is she still a vegetarian?

ALISON: Yes.

J.P.: You mean she eats fish?

44

ALISON: Yes.

J.P.: Ah yes. And chicken. There must be fifteen rooms in this house. I never understand why all one's guests huddle in the kitchen like prohibited immigrants.

ALISON: The dog's occupied the drawing room ever since I arrived.

CLIFF: How is she?

J.P.: There are those who prefer the company of pythons and grandchildren . . . She's gone.

CLIFF: I'm sorry.

J.P.: Teddy shall wear a black armband.

CLIFF: Oh God . . .

J.P.: (*To* ALISON) You can sit in there now if you wish. Still, I think the old thing deserves a little toast.
(*He pours three glasses. Hands one to each of them. Holds up the empty bottle.*)
I think we'll have some more of that. Well. (*Almost barks.*) Well – easy come. Easy go! (*To* ALISON) Off to your gig, then?

ALISON: I expect so.

J.P.: After coffee in the Rev. Ron's liturgical café? Well, I dare say an evening of Nuremberg Meatloafing will raise young Jim's persecuted spirit.

ALISON: At least it's not been tamed by dogs and snobby wines.

J.P.: Tamed? Tamed? Is that what you all think? (*To* CLIFF) Is it?

CLIFF: Chained up, a bit more like it. I can't say I've exactly walked to heel . . . yet. (*To* ALISON) You may be right about dogs. They do have this lurching instinct to please. It's there in all their little doggy sinew. Even unto death. Well, here's to her. No, you can't accuse J.P. of that. Performs in his fashion but never aims to please. Always had a friendly wag in there for most of us.

ALISON: It's not generally noticed.

CLIFF: You *might* say that about Teddy.

ALISON: I wouldn't say *anything* about fucking Teddy.

CLIFF: He doesn't approve of swearing.

J.P.: Who's paying for the tickets? Rev. Ron?

45

ALISON: I don't know.

J.P.: I understand they're snapped up at pretty snobby prices.

CLIFF: Alison, love, would you save my old feet? Get us some more of this? I reckon we'll be dining in tonight.

ALISON: Sure.

J.P.: Let's have the '65. We deserve it.

CLIFF: My feet don't. She's right about wine snobs.

J.P.: I know. The Nicaraguan '89 must be coming on nicely. Less taming.

ALISON: Right.

J.P.: Thank you.

(ALISON *goes out.*)

CLIFF: We'll have something exotic but simple to go with it. (*Crosses to a shelf lined with books.*) Let's have a look at all those chat-inducing books you never use.

J.P.: Tame. I should have thought smashing up churches was pretty tame. Nasty but tame. One of the ruins that Porter knocked about a bit. I didn't mind so much about the chancel screen. Late-Victorian Heal's restoration job. Inoffensive enough. I think everyone was delighted to see the end of that crapulous lectern bird by our friend Helena's mentor, Laugh-a-minute Lars Jasperson. Not a moment too soon.

CLIFF: (*Riffling through cookery books*) Or that huge Arts Council offering they both worked on.

J.P.: Oh. The one in the Winnie Mandela shopping precinct?

CLIFF: Dedicated to the spirit of Saint Gabriel.

J.P.: Gabriel, patron saint of postal, radio, telecommunications and telegraph and telephone, television operators. When I hear 'money for the arts', I reach for my Semtex plastic. (*CLIFF has caught sight of himself in the mirror.*)

CLIFF: Mirror, mirror on de wall, who am de fairest of dem all? (*J.P. casually takes out a leather-bound book from Alison's shoulder bag.*)

J.P.: (*Casually*) Snow White, you cocksucker.

CLIFF: Teddy thinks that's offensive.

J.P.: He mustn't expect cloying good taste in this establishment. If he's so downtrodden and loud-mouthed

46

about it, he shouldn't be so wafer-skinned. (*Turning the leaves of the book*) I suppose illiterates believe in some protocol of words. And candour breaks it.

CLIFF: Who said that?

J.P.: I did. No one.

CLIFF: Well, I wouldn't repeat it.

J.P.: You're right. My taste is going the way of my judgement.

CLIFF: You've marked a hell of a lot of these dishes. Ah, Italian. That looks good.

J.P.: I don't want any Welsh pasta, thank you. A lot of thought's gone into that cuisine.

CLIFF: I know – I've had an idea. What's that you've got?

J.P.: Young Alison's diary.

CLIFF: Wouldn't you say that was her private property?

J.P.: The great Jeremy Taylor said, 'Never ask what a man carries covered so curiously, for it is enough that it is covered curiously. Every man hath in his own life sins enough, in his own mind trouble enough and in performance his offices more than enough to entertain his own company.'

CLIFF: It's a nasty flaw in the minor masterpiece of your character.

(J.P. *flips through the diary throughout his speech.*)

J.P.: Exactly. Curiosity after the affairs of others cannot be without envy, and an evil mind. No, I wouldn't have minded the chancel and lectern so much. It was the memorial to poor Cornet Shanks VC. There was his marbled sword, breastplate and plumed shako and campaign medals. And its inscription: 'Cornet Shanks, son of the Right Hon. Timothy Shanks of this parish and Castle Tremlett – on the 20th February 1857, in a skirmish near Umkala, Cornet Shanks particularly distinguished himself when his captain was wounded by gallantly leading on his troop and twice and thrice charging a body of infuriated fanatics who had rushed on the guns shelling a small mud fort, killing three of the enemy with his own hand and incurring fifteen wounds of which he afterwards

47

died.' They actually took a sledgehammer to Cornet Shanks and smashed him to powder.

CLIFF: Well, he did die fighting infuriated fanatics. They just caught up with him.

J.P.: I can't see why Cornet Shanks should infuriate fanatics a hundred and fifty years on. Such spite for a simple soldier.

CLIFF: Teddy's colonial past is catching up with us.

J.P.: Young James, who can hardly lift the lemonade to pour into my malt, wielding a sledgehammer. I'd got fond of Cornet Shanks. A better man than our Anfony – or Jim – I should say.

CLIFF: Put her book away. It's private. I see you've marked this one up.

J.P.: Ah, deep waters here, you think? As expected, concerning a most empty seabed down below. (*Snaps the diary shut.*) Not much springtime in that little heart . . .

CLIFF: (*Reads*) 'I said I will take heed to my ways, that I offend not in my tongue. I will cup my mouth as it were a bridle.' Blimey, where's that?

J.P.: What?

CLIFF: Your bridle. 'While the ungodly is in my sight. I held my tongue and spake nothing. I kept silent, yea, even from good words.' When did we last hear a good word from you?

J.P.: Frequently. You didn't listen.

CLIFF: 'But it was pain and grief to me.'

J.P.: 'My heart was hot within me, and while I was thus musing the fire kindled: and at the last I spake with my tongue.' (*Enter* ALISON *with bottle of wine.*)

CLIFF: 'Let me know mine end, and the number of my days; that I may be certified how long I have to live.'

ALISON: 'Certified' is right.

CLIFF: 'And verily every man living is altogether vanity.'

ALISON: Man.

CLIFF: Sorry. Person 'walketh in a vain shadow: he heapeth up riches and cannot tell who shall gather them. And now, Lord, what is my hope: truly my hope is ever in thee.'

J.P.: You've caught Cliff in a Psalm situation, seeking guidelines. It's the morbid Methodism in him.

CLIFF: (*Returning the book to its shelf*) Only you would keep Cranmer next to Elizabeth David.

J.P.: The kitchen has its meaningful mysteries also. (*Hands ALISON the diary.*) Yours, I believe.

ALISON: Helena's arrived. Should I tell her to go?

J.P.: Ah, reinforcements. The Gay Gorgons are gathering. By no means. I'm afraid we'll bore you out, but she might find the Nicaraguan '89 amusing. There are still some brave causes left. (*Takes the wine from her. He sings a few lines quietly of 'If You were the Only Girl in the World'.*) I think that's probably the best song ever written.

ALISON: You would.

CLIFF: Better than Schubert.

J.P.: Oh, yes.

CLIFF: Strauss, Mahler.

J.P.: Different.

Tell me, do I take it that you are embarking on a brave new adventure?

ALISON: What do you mean?

J.P.: Becoming a one-parent family.

ALISON: It's none of your business.

J.P.: Quite. That was always a standby in the drama of my days. Last act: get the girl in the family way. It hardly poses the same dilemma now. I can't believe your heart was ever touched by something as flighty as a caprice. Still, sloth has its ways of striking back. Like young Jim and Cornet Shanks. I must go and reassure your friend that she is welcome in our vain shadow. (*Puts his fingers to his mouth.*) 'I will cup my mouth as it were a bridle.' Promise.

ALISON: Thanks.

(*The following, like the end of the scene, stretches the dangerous element of parody, even farce, to breaking point. But perhaps here in particular, it must be controlled so that both CLIFF and ALISON may repeatedly undercut J.P.'s more lyrical flights without diminishing him, still allowing him to remain intact. It requires a delicate delivery from the actors and, above all, the overriding force of irony, to carry him through the snares of ridicule.*)

J.P.: You ask for hope that is in no one's gift. Certainly not mine. You wouldn't come to me.

ALISON: You're joking.

J.P.: Yes. Hope does not feign feeling it cannot have.

ALISON: Don't patronize me, *Dad*.

J.P.: It doesn't dissemble or explain what is unknowable.

ALISON: Don't bother.

J.P.: It is deaf to comfort and counselling.

ALISON: You *are* deaf.

J.P.: To those who believe their heart strings are not in place to be struck and broken . . .

ALISON: You're broken, broken and washed up.

J.P.: . . . but can be – restructured is the word – by experts and crack Samaritans.

ALISON: Good and past it. We've had anger. Now it's the line on hope.

J.P.: I may be mangy, Alison, mangy, disordered but tame, tame I am not.

ALISON: Sorry!

J.P.: It suffers degradation that seems oh, infinite. And *not* always silently.

ALISON: You can say that again.

J.P.: But forgivingly.

ALISON: Forgiving. You!

J.P.: It might turn out to be my only virtue.

ALISON: No sign of it yet.

J.P.: When I was a little older than you –

ALISON: A packet of fags, a plate of Yorkshire pudding and a pint of beer all for fourpence. Even Teddy's heard that.

J.P.: The Testament of the New, you might say, did seem to have the merest edge in my restricted life. But now the Old, vengeful and warlike, has clouded over, darker than night or death because it must be *lived*.

CLIFF: (*Yawning*) I don't have to spell it out, Alison.

ALISON: Please. Don't. It's of no interest to me.

CLIFF: J.P.'s fairly potty at present. Aren't you?

J.P.: Barking.

ALISON: He always was.

CLIFF: And pissed. But not biting. Just at his own lead. Aren't you, Lord Sandy? Old thing? Young, grey-haired dodo?

ALISON: He *is* worse. You know he is.

CLIFF: It's only madness. Only nowadays they call it stress. It's just old-fashioned madness like we always had. There's a new, virulent strain, that's all.

ALISON: I know. There's a lot of it about.

CLIFF: Listen to his tone of voice, observe his demeanour. Is that the image of a madman?

J.P.: I'll smack your legs in a minute.

ALISON: Don't *you* get caught.

CLIFF: Tell us one of your feeble jokes, sing us your boring little songs. If you must. No, don't.

J.P.: It falters but never fawns or crowds, stands in line or even *waves*. Even in dread and noise, *your* youthful noise, tame, timid and commonplace. It strains for a snatch of harmony.

CLIFF: Oh, doesn't 'e go on! Poor old dad.
(J.P., *quiet, smilingly delivers the following at great speed and precision, as of recitative:*)

J.P.: All of which, my dear, is as unclear to you as it is to me as I say it. Barking. An old trumpet, cornet, trumpet, played upon but not playing. Hearing but only in my head. But, coherence isn't all, coherence, like the intellect of your mother's friends, conceals as much as is revealed to the lost like me who contemplate the wreckage. To be alone and not demand the light, *that* dear, one-parent-family Alison –

ALISON: Words. Stupid words.

J.P.: Language! – that only is goodness, gaiety, unapproved, unlegislated, unscaled, that is life, triumph, victory and dominion . . . (*To* CLIFF) You know, Whittaker – I *am* foolish. I must remember to breathe when I speak.
(J.P. *goes out. Blackout.*)

SCENE 2

The same. Some time has elapsed. CLIFF *and* J.P. *are both seated on either side of the table, centre. Below them, in the comfortable, unkitchenlike armchairs, are* ALISON *and* HELENA, *sprawled and immersed in the 'quality' newspapers.* J.P. *is reading a Murdoch tabloid with huge headlines, smoking his pipe with genuine enjoyment, and the lamp above the table creates a billiard-room cavern of smoke and light upon all their faces.*

HELENA *is a handsome girl, rather older than* ALISON, *muscular and speedy-looking, both in body and intelligence. Charm is a word she would abhor but she has an undoubted, natural magnetism which beckons imagination. The occasional blast of a sporting gun outside punctuates the earlier action.*

CLIFF, *wearing an apron, is still concentrated on the Book of Common Prayer. On the Aga are several saucepans, simmering gently, their steam mingling with the smoke from J.P.'s pipe.* HELENA, *downstage right from them, turns her face in mild irritation.*

J.P.: (*Presently*) Who would you rather sleep with?
    (*No response. He looks up.*)
    Who would you rather sleep with?
CLIFF: Please, James, not that.
J.P.: Who would you rather sleep with? Shirley Bassey or Margaret Drabble?*
CLIFF: Help!
J.P.: You've *got* to choose.
CLIFF: I don't. Oh, I don't think I could bear those Tiger Bay armpits.
J.P.: Bigot.
CLIFF: All right. Margaret. Nice, intellectual cuddle.
J.P.: Sexist.

*In the playing of the game Who Would You Rather? names may be substituted according to the prejudices and fashions of the day and locality.

52

CLIFF: (*To the girls*) You can't win this silly game.

J.P.: That's right. Who would you rather sleep with? Joan Collins or Joan Plowright?

CLIFF: Myrna Loy.

J.P.: That's not what you were asked. Meryl Streep or Snow White?

CLIFF: Snow White.

J.P.: You would. Fay Weldon or the Seven Dwarfs?

CLIFF: *Not* disadvantaged people?

J.P.: Glenys Kinnock or Ben Elton? Colonel Gadaffi or Yasser Arafat?

CLIFF: Well, I've heard of laying a tablecloth . . .

J.P.: Come on. Imagine you're a hostage.

CLIFF: Sometimes I think I am.

J.P.: Jane Fonda or –

CLIFF: Jane Fonda.

J.P.: You haven't heard the alternative. Jean Rook.

CLIFF: There. I was right. I don't see what this has to do with the global struggle between hate and love, greed and peace, oppressors and the oppressed.

ALISON: Who's Jean Rook?

CLIFF: There you are. You're mixing up categories. It should be for tragedy, comedy, history, pastoral, pastoral-comical, historical-pastoral –

J.P.: All right, here's one for all of you.

CLIFF: They're not interested.

J.P.: Who would you sleep with? Myra Hindley or Lord Longford?

CLIFF: Bad taste.

J.P.: Would I break faith with that? It's quite harmless.

CLIFF: You've upset Teddy.

J.P.: All right, girls. Some easy ones for you. Roy Hattersley or Barry Manilow? Very well. Jeffrey Archer or fragantly, downwardly, thrustingly Mrs A?

CLIFF: All the best ones are dead. Anti-racist-pastoral, gay-right-surbanites, rapist-inner-citical . . .

J.P.: Bob Monkhouse – or Sir Peter Hall?

CLIFF: Bruce Forsyth or Quasimodo?

J.P.: Noddy or Little Black Sambo.

CLIFF: The Rev. Ron or the Bishop of Bromley?

J.P.: Too close too home.

CLIFF: Saatchi and Saatchi or Little and Large?

J.P.: Anyone called Kevin or Wayne.

CLIFF: Or Debbie or Trish. I know: John Arden *and* Margaretta D'Arcy *or* the Beverly Sisters.

HELENA: I thought you didn't like games.

J.P.: I don't. Here's one for you, Helena.

CLIFF: Keep it.

J.P.: Andrew Neil or Paul Boateng?

HELENA: It's a rather cruel, pointless game.

CLIFF: He's not at his best today. Anyway, you're dead right. Here's another good one. (*Reading*.) 'He that begetteth a fool doeth it to his sorrow, and the father of a fool hath no joy.' Proverbs.

J.P.: A stiff prick hath no conscience – Thomas Aquinas. Put that bloody book away. It causes enough trouble.

CLIFF: You really shouldn't – that's another for Teddy's swear box. Not in front of ladies. Time we dished up. Come on, boyo, what's got into you? Be useful instead of sitting there failing to come up with solutions. You've been quite good up to now. Decant the Château North–South divide. Get busy. It's all right, girls. Stay as you are. The Great God Goddess Aga Person calls. Born to demand, to dominate. (CLIFF *goes to the Aga*.) Do you think Teddy's got BO?

J.P.: Palpably. (*Sniffs*.) Ah, the unmistakable, underfunded ambience of the Royal Court. BO, pot and bargain breaks at the gay sweatshop. I'm reminded of the young constable who arrested my son. I asked him how he felt about policing demonstrations like the ones favoured by Alison and her brave little brother. He said: 'I don't mind the banners hurled at your eyeballs, even the tormenting of the horses. It's that trampling cloud of BO.'

CLIFF: No. I'll bet you could eat your TV dinner out of Teddy's armpits.

J.P.: What better place?

CLIFF: He must be allowed to express himself. His armpits may be just a beginning to self-determination, to recognition of his cultural identity.

J.P.: Oh, I do recognize it. I do. And armpit shall speak unto armpit . . . (HELENA *has stepped up her attempts to fan away the smoke and steam within. She coughs.*)

CLIFF: That stinking old pipe.

J.P.: Shut up.

CLIFF: Why don't you do something? Poor Helena, look at her. She's choking.

J.P.: I'm sorry.

CLIFF: So you should be. We're just about to eat. Didn't you read the sign (*i.e.* THANK YOU FOR NOT SMOKING)?

J.P.: Yes. The hand of Teddy, I thought. Do you suppose that heaven's been designated a no-smoking area?

CLIFF: Well, it does sound like the General Synod's idea of the Good News. You'll have to knock that stinking thing out on them pearly gates before you're allowed through. Can't have all them little cherubim keeling over from passive smoking. Can't you see St Peter putting out his gnarled old fisherman's arm: 'Sorry, J.P. you can't bring that thing in here.'

J.P.: Indeed. Peter Prig's paradise. No élitist caviare to the sound of trumpets any more.

CLIFF: All that swept away ages ago. It'll be like the BBC. 'I'm afraid if you wish to smoke – '

J.P.: It'll have to be the other place. (*He starts to refill his pipe.*)

CLIFF: Picking up fag ends for eternity. Still, you'll meet a better class of person.

J.P.: A Lucifer to light my fag.

HELENA: What *do* you get out of it? Look at it. All that smugness and deliberation, the little knives, the petty ritual.

J.P.: You mean there's no longer ritual in heaven? Just committees and people calling themselves chairs?

CLIFF: What do you suppose the French will do? After all, their chairs are feminine. Do what they always do, I suppose.

J.P.: They'll *all* speak English. German American. Australian.

Chill-cooked English. (*To* HELENA) There's spirituality in a pipe, rarely in love and occasionally in friendship.

HELENA: You really are slipping, J.P., aren't you?

J.P.: Yes. It may not be the general experience but it's *mine*, however foolish it may seem to you, Helena. Half a century of convivial smoke.

HELENA: Convivial! Filthy, you mean?

J.P.: Yes, filthy and fetid, unhygienic, the swirling anticipation of people gathered together, the blue mist of Collins and the Hackney Empire . . .

HELENA: O God!

J.P.: The brasserie and bars, the music-halls of Sickert and La Goulu, lungs filling with carbon and laughter and recklessness, defying clinical death and a few unknowable extra years of antiseptic, germ-banished, senior citizen's golden retirement and pensions schemes.

CLIFF: *You'll* be old one day. You see.

J.P.: I doubt it. (*Spoken in an almost soothing bedside manner.*) But, if I am propped up on state pillows, being cathetized and patronized by some hell's angel of check-out mercy, young Nurse Noylene, I shall rise like some last-gasp Lazarus of a bygone smoke-filled civilization; I shall rise from my bed of unheeding profligacy and if any frowning *Gauleiter* breathes their concern or care over my fetid and exhausted form, or any smarmy dietician dares lay her menu of lower-middle-class mush, asking old Mr Porter what putrid filth he'd like to pass through his National Health dentures for his dinner at noon – if –

CLIFF: (*To the girls*) All memories of his hernia operation.

J.P.: (*Sweetly*) If anyone, any of these creeping refuse collectors, should refer to me as a senior citizen, they will get one last almighty smack in their sanitized mealy fucking mouth.

CLIFF: Swear box!

J.P.: When I was Junior, Junior Porter, I spake as a child, a child of hellfire and smoke, within and without, I swore to the gods of irreverence and dissent that even then spake within me: I will never –

ALISON: Be a member of the public. We know.

56

HELENA: Not even in the blue and golden days and nights of smoke?

J.P.: A member of the congregation.

HELENA: Ah.

J.P.: But no matey handshakes either. Alone and among many. Senior I am not. Senior to what? To whom? Seniority, the campaign medal of the dull and cowardly. I am certainly not a citizen of the UK. Sounds like belonging to the Co-op. Underwashed, underendowed, unappealing, un-United Kingdom. All right for her Britannic Majesty's cry of football curs and the red and peeling beery spies, in their battalions, throwing up at Spanish skies.

CLIFF: Snobby, snobby, Lord Sandy.

ALISON: Time you retired, Dad.

J.P.: Retirement, ah the red badge of mediocrity.

CLIFF: He *used* to have a nice way with words. But I'm afraid he's losing it. It's talking down to Teddy.

ALISON: No one ever accused *you* of originality.

J.P.: No. But I don't assemble a lot of sloppy fads and serve them up as innovations. Do you know that before Auntie Wordsworth retired from his serious scribbling, people in their coaches used to pull down the blinds so that they didn't need to contemplate the landscape? In the previous century, no one would have known what you meant by *Angst* or even anxiety. As for boredom – no one felt that before the Russians droned on about it.

HELENA: And what perception have *you* invented?

J.P.: None I can remember. Just perhaps the abiding expectation that more change means less improvement.

CLIFF: The only things that have improved in my lifetime are medicine and dentistry. Try to shut up, you'll put the girls off my nicely prepared rebuke to the sluttish British housewife.

(*Sings the the tune 'Lucky Ole Sun':*)

    Sluts in the kitchen,
    Sluts in the bed,
    Sluts in their every sweet way,
    But whatever you do,

They roll around heav'n all day.
Are you sure there's nothing on the box?

J.P.: What's the matter with him? (*Points to Teddy.*)

CLIFF: He's just becoming more and more unsure of his self-worth. That's all.

J.P.: That's all. Tough titty, Teddy.

CLIFF: What it comes down to –

J.P.: Down to what?

CLIFF: He's suffering from stress.

J.P.: Rats suffer from stress. They don't *suffer*.

HELENA: Like you?

J.P.: I endure. Energetically, I hope to God, and with some grace and a snatch of unregarded wit. What your tight-arse, average sloth likes to call self-pity. I don't think Teddy's too solid flesh is going to melt before our eyes. That bear should go on a diet.

CLIFF: Perhaps he does suffer. How do you know?

J.P.: Let him earn it.

HELENA: Earn? Why must he earn?

J.P.: What you'd call input. We mustn't forget his rights, must we?

CLIFF: After all, he *is* –

J.P.: A human being?

CLIFF: He can't be blamed for trying to be.

J.P.: Teddy has a very anthropomorphic glitter. He's really not very interesting.

HELENA: Hear, hear!

J.P.: And, as a character, ultimately *un*convincing. The truth, my good friends, is both breathtaking and obvious. Teddy is a cunt. A cunt and replete with cant.

CLIFF: Well, we know you don't really mean that. You're very fond of him.

J.P.: I am. He's a cunt. A forcibly cant-fed cunt. Teddy – give us a lovely soft wet kiss.

CLIFF: You've probably all noticed he keeps mumbling about the Protestant Work Ethic.

J.P.: He does. He would.

CLIFF: Be fair.

J.P.: Why?

HELENA: Why not?

J.P.: Why dissemble?

CLIFF: All he wants is to help create a better and more just society.

J.P.: Surely.

CLIFF: And participate in it.

J.P.: Let him.

CLIFF: At least he's trying. All right, his targeting in on a few, maybe pithy, turns of popular phrase may be a little naive.

J.P.: He's all pith, our Teddy, and to no great moment.

CLIFF: Yeth.

J.P.: Picking up your cues nicely. It must be the Chilean *rosé* I slipped into your chalice. He's no Protestant. As for ethic, he's probably confused it with 'ethnic', another impeccably kosher word. Or got someone else's teeth in. Anyway, tell him to stop it.

CLIFF: You tell him.

J.P.: Why?

CLIFF: You're the eldest.

J.P.: Oh?

CLIFF: You have authority.

J.P.: Never. He'll listen to *you*. That class like it best from their own kind, kith or pith, whatever, anyway, NCOs like your dear self.

CLIFF: Actually when I did my National Service, they told me I was prime officer material.

J.P.: Did they? What regiment was that? Jewish Rifles?

CLIFF: I was Leading Aircraftman – *as* you well know. He does.

J.P.: Very fetching you must have looked. All Brylcreem, acne and camp concert tutu. No wonder we were trounced at Suez.

CLIFF: It was long before that. He's relying on you not knowing.

J.P.: Or caring. It's mere history. And recent at that. I'm accustomed to your Swansea-terrace ignorance. There he is – the spokesperson of illiteracy spread for generations from the staff rooms of our teacher training colleges.

CLIFF: I was a prize graduate.

J.P.: You were. You are. A tribune of the British Playground.

CLIFF: I was before comprehensives. He knows that.

J.P.: You mean it went downhill *after* they chucked you out? That third-class degree didn't help so much in them days.

CLIFF: I didn't have a third-class degree. *He* only got a poor Second.

J.P.: It was the only acceptable and only stylish one. It combined natural modesty with a refusal to strive for commonplace ambitions. Only monkey-witted little strivers got Firsts. Department of first-class minds.

CLIFF: Those things don't matter. What he's trying to acquire is communications' skills.

J.P.: I'll bet your pupils all called you Cliff.

CLIFF: I was addressed as 'Mr Lewis'.

J.P.: Ah, not 'sir'?

CLIFF: I drew the line at that.

J.P.: When you were trying to deprive the little Zulus of their Stanley knives, or was it bicycle chains in them gentler days of free milk and the odd traumatic caning? No wonder you didn't last.

CLIFF: There's nothing wrong with the system.

J.P.: Apart from the results we live with here. Oh dear, soppy-headed louts like you wheedling away to the New Scum.

CLIFF: Oh, he's got a cruel tongue.

HELENA: You think your son should go for a poor Second?

J.P.: Ah, young Jim – he will have the comfort – and he will strive for it – of a pass in joined-up writing, Black Studies, most keen and encouraging to us all, and maybe Gay Engineering, social or otherwise, thrown in. Effortless mediocrity is a little beyond young James. He must be nurtured to it. This is all Teddy's fault. It's his mooing on about the Protestant Work Ethic. If only they'd bring back the barrel organ. Such a pretty sound. He and young James are not under-achievers. In his own case he's just a dumb, no-talent, albeit, animal. Of small account and less interest.

CLIFF: He only wants to learn –

J.P.: No, he doesn't. He wants, God save us all, to express

himself. Above all, like children, he must be utterly discouraged at any attempts at self-expression. Let him accept the fact and leave us all and himself in peace. He has nothing to offer.

CLIFF: Perhaps – he could be an alternative comedian.

J.P.: A substitute for laughter. He could. Now, let's turn our attention to other things. (*From* Radio Times *or* TV Times) Here's an enthusiastic reader's letter: 'Dear Sir, I had frankly never heard of Oscar Wilde . . .'

CLIFF: What group is that?

J.P.: The ignorance that's proud to speak its name. 'I had frankly never heard of Oscar Wilde but I thoroughly enjoyed Sunday night's play. What gay people had to endure in less enlightened days! Could you tell me what books I could get out of the library about him?'

HELENA: Fat chance, these days.

J.P.: 'Or better still, a series?' I think perhaps Oscar Fingal O'Flahertie Wills might have found Reading less offensive than rapturous membership of something calling itself a community. Better to suffer in Athens than glory in Thebes.

CLIFF: I know; who would you rather: Lord Alfred Douglas or –

J.P.: They don't like that fatuous game.

CLIFF: Well, tell us a joke if you won't shut up. Best of all, shut up and give me a hand. What about the one about the Bishop and the pink blancmange?

J.P.: That only makes *me* laugh and *I* heard it when I was seven. Anyway, I don't tell jokes any more. Not in front of ladies. A good woman of the meagrest spirit or intelligence can destroy a joke between the eyes of a gnat at a hundred yards. My first wife wasn't half a bad marksperson.

HELENA: (*To* ALISON) Why do you come back to this madhouse?

J.P.: The Rev. Ron doesn't have an ironing board. He thinks they're a symbol of male dominance, like Our Father, which may be up in the Happy Non-Smoking Zone beyond.

CLIFF: Come on, daddy blue-eyes, help me dish up.
(*They do so,* J.P. *pouring the wine first. The meal should be simple but with a show of formality. Little quails. Bread, cheese and salad.*)
CLIFF: Our vegetarians. No fish or chicken, I'm afraid.
HELENA: Thank you.
CLIFF: There is a chicken's Auschwitz up the road. But J.P. never uses it . . . The quails now, *they've* been shot so I know you wouldn't fancy them.
HELENA: They do seem to have a happy Sunday, banging away.
CLIFF: The brutal ways of country folk.
J.P.: First, there's the tactical softening up.
CLIFF: He's back on joke abuse. Sing us a song, if you must. Must be nearly Mother's Day. What about (*sings*):
  It's my mother's birthday today:
  I'm on my way with a lovely bouquet.
  That's very moving.
J.P.: 'No, darling, before you start the story, it *wasn't* Christmas Eve it was Good Friday.' Does it make any difference? 'No, but you might as well get it right. And, actually it was Jowett who first said it.' That's just a preliminary rattle to your verve. Then, during the actual telling, there are the follow-up blows on selected targets. 'Darling, I'm sorry to interrupt but I think Philippa's glass is empty.' Mountains and memory move. Right. 'Oh, before you go on, Frank needs an ashtray. Sorry, darling, do go on. It's very funny when he tells it well.'
CLIFF: Right, come on, girls. Grub up!
J.P.: There you are! *He's* doing it.
(*The girls move to the table and sit down.*)
CLIFF: It only works well when he gets the mime right.
J.P.: Up she gets, refilling already brimming glasses, plumping cushions, thrusting unneeded ashtrays.
CLIFF: Like Alison at her dressing table.
J.P.: Piss off. Eventually, the end comes, just as the paltry little punchline hurtles into sight, all but intact. It comes, the cobra strike of her hand on the poker. And, yes, she pokes the fire, not as you and I poke it, but she explodes into the

embers. There is a silence and she looks up in wifely bafflement. 'Oh, I'm sorry, darling. I thought you'd finished.' Your tiny quail of wit is blown from the sky.

HELENA: Perhaps the killer instinct for the Porter joke is just an aversion to a tired old routine of juggling with stereotypes?

J.P.: You've got it, Helena. Hasn't she?

HELENA: Like mothers-in-law.

J.P.: Listen, Helena, people strain, study, often at great public expense, to *become* stereotypes; to be home-buyers, high-up-there-flying executives, brief-case Boadiceas, tragic mums, anorexics. These roles are our right, made available to all. All members of the public, stereotypes all.

CLIFF: I'm a stereotype.

J.P.: You bet you are. Ellie certainly is. 'What made you choose that colour?'

CLIFF: I'm a very warm human person, rumbling with complexities.

J.P.: You're full of Celtic shit.

CLIFF: Teddy's a stereotype.

J.P.: He was *born* one. Born middle aged, creeping little cuddly conformist.

CLIFF: Bad parenting. Doesn't know what kind of stereotype he should refuse to be.

HELENA: (*To* J.P.) And you? Are you?

J.P.: Someone's working on it.

CLIFF: He's a hermit stereotype. Most unattractive.

HELENA: (*Lightly*) I've never heard two men sit around talking such bone-crunching balls.

CLIFF: Now then.

J.P.: There you are, Whittaker. I told you: I must learn to breathe when I speak.

HELENA: Am *I* a stereotype?

J.P.: No, Helena. I think you're an attractive, unusual, perceptive woman, nobody's fool and a bit anxious to prove it. You've just picked up some bad language, all the dumb pieties of the progressives, futurologists and illiterates you have been unprivileged enough to grow up among.

CLIFF: Come on, it'll get cold. Not a punchline in sight.

J.P.: (*Pouring wine*) You corrupt and you call it caring.

HELENA: Why *do* you reach for the Semtex when you hear the word 'culture'?

J.P.: (*Sharply*) I am saying that there may, only may, be an order of precedence of arts and skills, like marine navigation, astronomy, sonata form, cabinet and clock making, gothic revival, horse racing, tapestry, oratorio, *The Tempest* and Turner and between, let us say, not unfairly, limbo, break dancing and dreadlock, rapping and pugilism, soul food and music, calypso and oil drum, *Robinson Crusoe*, Sugar Ray Robinson. Well, so much for culture.

CLIFF: (*Sighing*) Oh dear, what a mellow fellow you've become.

HELENA: You shit.

J.P.: Pass me one of the posh papers, will you? Gossip, that's what we want. Now there's a cultured art. Thank you, Helena. Ah. Do you know *I* invented these.

HELENA: You.

J.P.: *I* coined the phrase 'Posh Papers'.

HELENA: Fancy. You have your footnote in history after all.

J.P.: Oh, nobody knows. Oh yes, at the end of the day, they took it on board, seeking out the world's leaders and, sensitive to world opinion, they targeted in on it: Posh Papers.

HELENA: You identify it and, hey presto, it exists. Like a new strain of flea.

J.P.: I give to airy nothing a habitation and a name.

HELENA: Can you do it to people?

J.P.: Not really. Unless I can crack their motive. The quail is excellent, Whittaker.

CLIFF: Thank you, sir.

J.P.: Don't you think, Alison?

HELENA: The vegetables are terrific.

CLIFF: I was a vegetarian for a while. *He* was too. Gave it up same time as the banjo.

J.P.: Life is terrible and death is worse. There's the gravy so don't ask anyone to pass it. Life is terrible and death is worse. You are unconnected to the past. Hopeless about the future. Let me put this idle little dinner-table doodle to you, Helena.

HELENA: Well?

J.P.: If a man says life is hell, he is thinking, 'God doesn't love me any more.' His wife, hearing this, says, 'My husband, doesn't love me any more.' His best friend thinks –

CLIFF: 'Poor old bugger. He never *was* very lovable.'

J.P.: The wife says to her husband, '*You* don't love me any more.' To which the man replies, 'I do love you. Of course I do. All I said was: Life is hell.' To which the woman replies, 'You wouldn't say that if you loved me.'

CLIFF: El Cheapo Teddy Award, I think, don't you, Helena?

J.P.: It doesn't require a response. I'm accustomed to the banging of uptipped seats.

HELENA: I've often wondered, what *did* you read at that White Tile University? What *was* it?

J.P.: Well, I tell you, Helena, it was what you might call the Explanation Schools. I learned what marked a poet down as 'minor', what made a masterpiece flawed, observed the course of the class struggle as structured in the *Beano* and the *Dandy* and why a university graduate should be running a sweet stall. Discuss. Where were we? Oh yes, culture. (*Grabs a dictionary from among the cookery books.*) Panacea, Polytechnic, Pusillanimous.

CLIFF: What does that mean?

J.P.: What?

CLIFF: Pusillanimous.

J.P.: How do *I* know? It's not a word I'd ever use. Wrong volume. A to M. Albigensian, Buggery, Chauvinist, blimey, aggressive patriotism. Here we are, Culture: 'enlightenment or refinement arising from artistic values and pursuit of excellence'. 'Acquainting ourselves with the best that has been known and said' – Matthew Arnold. Here's Auntie Wordsworth: 'Where grace of culture has been utterly unknown.' Poor old bugger. *He* got it all wrong.

CLIFF: Well, not very multicultural, Grasmere, in them days. All that tranquillity sounds fair hell.

J.P.: Here. Not facing up to the exciting potential of the Industrial Revolution.

CLIFF: Steam, coal, iron, cotton. No apprehension of the satanic mills, the envy of the world, just cloud-capped hills and dozy daffodils, ventureless, privileged, private world.

J.P.: Hell. If a man says life is hell –

CLIFF: Pass me the poker, Alison.

J.P.: If a man says life is hell to an American, he replies. What?

CLIFF: Does it matter?

J.P.: 'You've got a problem.' If he says it to a Frenchman, he replies, 'In French, this means nothing.' To a Welshman, life is hell?

CLIFF: 'But not in Wales.'

J.P.: To an Irishman –

CLIFF: 'Brits Out.'

J.P.: To Dr Dreadlocks: 'It's the legacy of colonialism.' To a socialist: 'It's cruel, uncaring Thatcherism.'

CLIFF: The Tory says: 'Privatize it.'

J.P.: And the feminist? Helena?

HELENA: Pass *me* the poker.

J.P.: 'The tyranny of men.'

CLIFF: Can we have the France–Wales match on, captain?

J.P.: No.

HELENA: You know what you two sound like? A pair of lovers. Befuddled old lovers.

J.P.: Yes, it was always a commonplace assumption. Especially among women and Americanos. I think Ellie gave it a lot of thought, don't you?

CLIFF: She never mentioned it. (*To* HELENA) He was always very camp, mind you. When nobody knew what that was.

HELENA: And were you?

CLIFF: Lovers?

J.P.: Good heavens, no. He's far too plain. Aren't you, dreamboat?

CLIFF: But very kissable.

J.P.: Oh yes – Miss Tongue Sandwich. Like a beery labrador.

CLIFF: Teddy's more of a dry kisser.

HELENA: Oh, not Teddy.

CLIFF: Yes, you really must stop being so camp. It's dated and it never really suited your vapid personality. Besides, you bring odium on the gay community.

J.P.: Fuck the gay community.

CLIFF: Now then!

J.P.: A sensitive writer from Arden
    Sucked thespians off in his garden
    Said: I can't get enough
    Of this heavenly stuff
    While Thatcherite tyrannies harden.
(*Gulps*.) . . . Pardon. To think that when I lay in the Anderson shelter, suffering the abuses of the Hun, from the suburban ashes of ration books and sweetie coupons would rise Teddy's new almighty army, the unstoppable LMC.

HELENA: (*To* CLIFF) What's LMC?

CLIFF: Lower middle class. The likes of him. Born not in a trunk but in a three-piece suite. Not a picture on the walls nor a book in sight. Poor Jim, James laid waste by junk, junk persons, children, junk ending all. All he can do is pretend it isn't happening.

J.P.: Even doggerel has its insights.
    A sodomite playwright named Tich
    And a most irredeemable bitch
    Said: I've given up cocks
    To sleep outdoors in a box
    It's the *last* word in radical kitsch.

CLIFF: You're all washed up, Gaylord, you know that?

J.P.: For this craven Welsh wisdom much thanks.

HELENA: Your friend's right.

J.P.: Are you ganging up on me?

CLIFF: Yes.

J.P.: Well, that's all right. Complaining is *not* endearing. We must take what comes. Rise above it.
    Young gays undergoing analysis
    Say: Straights just *don't know* what malice is
    And with anal dilatation appalling the nation
    They cling to their stiffening fallacies.

I *shall* try to improve. Promise. (*He raises his glass.*)

CLIFF: Excellent. (*To* HELENA) You've had a chastening effect on him.

J.P.: My complaints are but the cries of severed enthusiasms.

CLIFF: Think of the torpor we endured in them sweet-stall days. No 1992 round the corner, the twenty-first century all but half a century away. A lifetime before the race to run. Look forward, beyond yourself. Don't look down, but above all, not back. Turn again, Porter. You shall thrice be Lord Lower Middle Classes.

J.P.: You don't seem to have done much looking back at this quail.

CLIFF: Job Porter's complaint.

J.P.: I'm sorry, but it's barely warm.

CLIFF: It's the Great God Aga.

J.P.: It's Alison's mother. My first wife's. Not *hers*. Though it could be. It's numero uno. Come to haunt. It's her mouldering rhino spirit. (*Bangs Aga with poker.*) Are you in there? Can you hear me, Mother?

CLIFF: No swearing. Not in front of ladies.

J.P.: I shouldn't think they'd care to be called that.

CLIFF: Or I shall go back to London. You never used to swear.

J.P.: No.

CLIFF: Not even when you were angry.

J.P.: I *was* quoting, actually.

CLIFF: It's a bit desperate when you start plagiarizing yourself.

ALISON: Hear, hear.

J.P.: I'd say massive reputations were built on it.

CLIFF: Be positive, innovative, invent.

J.P.: Be original? Not much market there, Whittaker. Like modesty.

CLIFF: Think of something.

HELENA: No more limericks, please.

J.P.: Ah, the poor sonnets of irreverence. We need a new vocabulary of swearing. Fresh words.

CLIFF: He had, Alison, quite a way with words once, didn't you, captain?

J.P.: I equivocated quite prettily.

CLIFF: Wouldn't know it now. Poor old thing.

J.P.: It was the tone of voice. But no one got it.

CLIFF: People found it hard to know when they were being confided in or insulted. We need a new swear word.

J.P.: You may do.

CLIFF: Instead of all those LMC profanities. I know: what about, Solomon Isaacs.

J.P.: I think that's already been used. Sollocks.

CLIFF: *You* think of something.

J.P.: Salman Rushdie.

CLIFF: Yes. That sounds quite rude. Salman Rushdie. Sushdie. Quite filthy really.

J.P.: Alison's mother pitched into me because I reproved some woman at someone else's dinner party.

ALISON: I remember. She was also one of Mummy's best friends.

J.P.: Most famous friends. Told me she was a research psychologist at East London Polytechnic. Lived in a collective in Kilburn, edited the *Harpies' Left Review*. She threw pots.

ALISON: She's a very distinguished potter.

CLIFF: Sushdie damnit.

J.P.: I think that may be in bad taste. She was deep into Scottish folk dancing, the peace movement, and she and her husband wrote children's books together.

CLIFF: That's enough. Sushdie!

J.P.: She left in tears halfway through the brown rice and Mummy said how could I insult anyone in such a way in someone else's house. I said, where else could I insult her? I'd never *have* her in my house. I think the real reason she was angry was that they were both famous. Her mama only dines with the famous, gives parties, lunch or love to the famous –

CLIFF: Something you'll never be.

J.P.: – famous, distinguished, oh yes, Mummy's clever. What an abiding embarrassment I must have been to her. I caught her discussing Croatian verb endings with some

First Secretary once. The good old rattle of first-class minds. Poor muddle-headed Jimmy, she called me.

CLIFF: You should have stayed down among the three-piece suites. You'd have been happier. And called your daughter Beverley, Belinda or Sharon.

J.P.: Alison was in worst taste.

HELENA: Why *did* you call her Alison?

J.P.: Actually her mother was behind it. It made her feel generous about the failure of my first marriage. She does thrive on feeling sorry for people. You've met her.

HELENA: She *does* greet you always as if you've just suffered a bereavement.

J.P.: Quite. Or are about to.

HELENA: (*Feeling disloyal*) Sorry, Alison.

ALISON: (*Shrugs.*) It's just Mummy's way. She's only wanting to help.

J.P.: Who needs her –

CLIFF: Sushdie – !

J.P.: What gossip have I got for you? A lot's happened since you were here last. Apart from young Jim's attempted arson and wholesale destruction, but he's really an outsider. I only learnt last week that the top sidesman wears ladies' underclothes. His wife runs the post office. Apparently, these things on the line are his not hers. I did think they're rather large. Everyone's amazed that Mrs Price didn't win first prize for the best home-made fruit cake for the fifth time running. I must say, so am I. If you stay for tea you can have some. Not like news from Chile or Czechoslovakia but it gives me something to think about. Lots of sex round here. Not much violence. Drunkenness, yes. The pubs seem to stay open all hours and the police crowd outside them like the SAS watching Mrs Thatcher. There's a certain amount of growing concern about poor Captain Shanks.

HELENA: Fancy.

J.P.: They're getting up a fund to put him back together again. Gave 'em a fiver. I may not be hot on brave causes but I know a more-or-less good one.

HELENA: You think so? It seems to me you've never made an honest decision in your life.

J.P.: Honest indecision –

HELENA: Feebleness.

J.P.: Complaining may not be admirable but it's better than sanctimony.

HELENA: Ah, the old dog's lost all the teeth it ever had. Regretting things it never had or never were. Spitting scorn on your wives who've both left you and now on your children, who are just about to. Have you thought about what *you've* done or, rather, haven't done?

J.P.: Little else. But you're right.

HELENA: I wish you'd stop agreeing with me.

J.P.: How beautiful you are when you're angry.

CLIFF: Oh, El Cheapo.

J.P.: Mistake. I'd given up paying compliments to ladies. The wateriest smile. I idly admired the frock of one of Alison's friends the other day and she looked as if she was off howling to the rape centre. But you must admit, Helena's looking splendid. Like a cat with a bird in its mouth.

HELENA: Thank you.

J.P.: As you know, I don't much care for cats.

HELENA: No. Slobbering, grateful old dogs.

J.P.: Like all selfish creatures, cats have no manners. Do you know the most odious word in the English language?

HELENA: I can think of two. Both proper nouns.

J.P.: Foreplay. Foreplay. A word of most feminine extraction. Cloying, charmless and rapacious . . . (*To* CLIFF) Do you remember that girl who opened that pulse-food – organic-food place up the road.

CLIFF: Red hair, woolly cap? Lucinda.

J.P.: Lucinda. Lucinda-Down-on-your-Left I called her. Her husband tried to run some sort of art gallery as well. The shop did quite well but what with the M.o.D. clipping the hedges all around and the enthusiasms of all the peasantry here for the Falklands War, they were driven back to Camden Town. I honestly think the reactionary rural classes shocked them horribly. Like being slipped a Mickey

71

Finn of South African sherry. Now, *she* was *very* cat-like. In fact I told her – over some mulled East German wine in her studio at the back of the shop one afternoon. To my surprise, she didn't call me a filthy old flasher but agreed with me. She was, she said, a *very* cat person. In spite of their aristocratic, privileged associations. Lucinda intrigued me a bit. Apart from her abhorrence of Western Materialism, old Red Pussy fairly spat with contempt at the mere mention of men. They both seemed pretty well off to me. The husband didn't say a lot but he clearly agreed with everything she said. Anyway, one afternoon I bought a packet of lentils for the rabbit stew and followed Ms D.L. into the studio.

CLIFF: That's enough.

J.P.: Helena, you've cheered me up. She tripped it off at you like Mrs Danvers checking off the linen cupboard. Attributes. Male issue: aggressive, competitive, dominant, insensitive, brutal, rude. Female: gentle, compassionate, unwarlike, extreme tenderness and sensibility. She didn't really talk to you. It was as if she was always addressing the chair. I couldn't make out where all this impersonal dislike, even hatred came from. As you know, I'm accustomed to personal dislike.

CLIFF: Teddy likes you. Still.

J.P.: Which *can* be painful *and* disconcerting. Where did it all originate? She hardly knew me. Anyway, one afternoon, over the mulled workers' grape, she started to take her clothes off.

CLIFF: What about *Mr* Lucinda?

J.P.: I don't know. Being equal – if that's what he was – they had an ethic of unaccountability or something.

HELENA: I thought you boys didn't go in for powder-room tales.

J.P.: She's only a name in this company. Well, there she stood, in the buff, surrounded by sacks of split peas and whole-milled oats, very pale, with that dry, almost flaky skin some redheads have. So, I thought, well, it seemed impolite not to do the same. I stood there, feeling a little like someone about to have an enema administered by some naked Pre-Raphaelite nursing sister. Now I know that the male form has none of the secret allusiveness of the female. Only athletes or occasional boys escape ridicule. We are not, on the whole, an exhilarating lot to contemplate in the nude. I always feel that women are most discreet about it. I realized how rarely they *do* look at you. And then –

CLIFF: No details, please.

J.P.: She was one of nature's policemen. No, she was exactly like one of those car park attendants. You approach, hands on an uneasy wheel. And then comes the instructions, the drill. (*Mime sequence; parade-ground delivery:*) Right, down on your left. *Left*, I said. Hard down. Right. Down. No. No. Down. Start again. Back up. Back up, I said. Now, try the other. Left hand. Down, down, I said. Left. Oh, God. Haven't you ever done this before? Back up. Oh. You've *plenty* of room. You could park a double-decker bus in there. Now, come forward, forward. Forward, I said! Now right down, down. Have you no sense of direction? Co-ordination? Now, quickly, plenty of room. Don't hesitate. What *are* you doing! Careful, careful, no, no, not *that* way! Try again, come on, once more, I've never seen anything easier in my life. O God, you're *hopeless*! You'll never make it. You'd better try somewhere else. Get some practice . . . Go *on*! She's one of the new army. The multi-clitoral parking attendant.

CLIFF: O God. Who would you rather . . .

J.P.: Sushdie to you!

CLIFF: That's a swear word.

J.P.: Andrea Dworkin . . .

CLIFF: Take no notice of him, girls. He's had at least three women shot from under him. Haven't you, captain? Don't just sit there. The girls' glasses are empty.

J.P.: Ah, I'm sorry.

HELENA: Do you realize how ridiculous that little bit of mime makes *you* look?

J.P.: My dear, *I* was the butt of it. Do you think I *invented* Lucinda-Down-on-your-Left?

HELENA: No.

J.P.: That she never happened, doesn't exist?

HELENA: I was never very good at parking myself.

J.P.: Ah, you *are* a generous girl. I knew you were. Being a woman is a fine thing. I know, I *do* know. Some have been very kind to me. Patient beyond any expectations. You think I am flippant and unkind about Lucinda. I am not. It's just that, in her own little way, she blasphemes against every act of loyalty, friendship and attention – women have ever and quite often paid to the likes of myself. She is an agent provocateur, a fraudulent and wicked woman. She goes on about her gender and makes it sound as trivial as having a bad back. Stupid I am but fraudulent no. Whatever you may say, I have oppressed no one.

CLIFF: You've oppressed Teddy.

J.P.: Someone *has* to oppress him otherwise he wouldn't exist. I'm sorry about Lucinda. I didn't mean to bring her up.

HELENA: Didn't you?

J.P.: No. You know, Whittaker, not only must I learn to breathe when I speak, I *must* watch my inflexions. They are beginning to *plunge* horribly. We inhabit a world of dying inflexions, dragging down everything with them. Listen to young Jimmy. That downward fall of the voice. *Down*, like Lucinda. Alison's not so bad. Downwardly, boringly. Cliff's Welsh at least rises in complacency; if Aussies rise in suspicion, so do the Geordies for some gritty reason. But you, Helena, your voice rises like a kite on the heath. It has the drift of irony, vigour and courage. God, imagine waking up with the sound of the Midwest or Birmingham in your ears, or the tones of Debbie or Kevin on your pillow. (*In falling inflexion.*)

> What a piece of work is a man, how noble in reason, how infinite in faculties, in form and moving how express and admirable, in action how like an angel, in apprehension how like a god.

Shall I put you through now, caller? There go your high spirits if you ever had any, down, down.

CLIFF: It's getting late. I think I'll light the lamp. Mustn't get morbid.

J.P.: For every light on Broadway lies a broken heart.

CLIFF: Yes. Money doesn't buy happiness. And we've none of that.

J.P.: Ah, yes, the crimson twilight. It comes around quite soon. Don't go yet.

(*A car horn.*)

What's this then? A motor. (*Goes to the window.*) 'Tis but the Reverend Ron. I say, the Synod *has* done well by him. That's his second motor in a year. Well, he must be *mobile*. The inner city is a large parish, even though *we* don't inhabit it. He's getting out . . . left the liturgical cafeteria to look after itself. He's got one of those snappy little shirt dog-collars.

HELENA: Would you say you were a Christian?

J.P.: Not necessarily, Helena. Do you know there are people who have 'poet' inscribed in their passport? It does seem a trifle presumptuous. To call yourself a poet and sodomite is one thing, but *poet*. James Porter, poet, Christian and broadcaster. No, I think not. What do you suppose he's doing here, in the crimson twilight?

ALISON: He's come to pick up Jimmy's things.

J.P.: Ah yes, there he is with his AA book and the Good News Bible in the glove box with last year's red nose and comic hat in aid of mob philanthropy. And there's young Jimmy, to coin one of Teddy's phrases, keeping a low profile. Why did he bother to come at all, all pale and ill-used in the vicar's passenger seat? Is *that* the face of a generation whose aspiration and enthusiasms *I* have crushed?

HELENA: Yes.

J.P.: You should read our parish magazine and see what's going on at England's heart.

HELENA: Should I?

J.P.: Its hard-hitting editor is none other than our fearless young abductor, the Rev. Ron. And here he is, on the front page, beside the Chancel Roof Appeal, featuring our very own axe-happy iconoclast, young James, as the subject of this month's 'Ron Speaks with Christ' column. 'I should have liked to take as my talking point young James Porter, a personal friend of mine and a popular figure in our parish. However, Jim, as you all know, is at present in a spot of public bother, and I am unable to discuss his situation while the matter is *sub judice*. But it does allow me to bring to your attention the plight of similar young people all over our nation. Folk who are daily being driven to violence, acts of destruction and degradation, by evil forces and often through no fault of their own making. Take the widely reported case of Greville Plumb, a fourteen-year-old who ran away from home and family to hustle for a living in London, and was forced by sheer hunger to sell his only asset, his body, and was brutally, painfully, murdered. Either we push our young into the waiting arms of pimps and drug-pushers in the nearest metropolis, the criminal sub-culture that is lying in wait to exploit them; or we show them we need them, want them to stay and provide them with the prospect of a decent standard of living. To its credit our Church is showing at last that it really wants the young to be included in its life and worship. It is offering space for the young to meet (either in the church itself or in an annex to the Parish Room) – somewhere where they can play music, be themselves, and find their space. We should all give the PCC and the Parish Council every support in ending the cycle of deprivation and disenchantment to which the young have been subjected. NOW, before it's too late.' That's telling 'em. Well, it's past remedy, I'd say, wouldn't you? I'd say yoof custody was preferable to chat-along-a-Ron. Rather face the spears of Captain Shanks's deadly dervish than the plain pop chat of the parson. In the face of such things, Madam, I have become very Saracen. (*Sings verse of 'It's My Mother's Birthday Today . . .', 'With Laughing Irish Eyes'. Doorbell rings.* ALISON *rises.*)

My name is Jimmy Fucked-up Porter
It started with the Colonel's daughter.
A stranger still I stand afraid
Alone and in a world I never made. –

I'll go.
(*As he goes off singing.*)
    My heart is singing a happy refrain
    Blue skies are smiling above.
(*Waves.*)
    I'm going home to my mother again
    Off to the one that I love.
(*Exit. Off:*)
    It's my mother's birthday today
    I'm on my way with a lovely bouquet . . .
CLIFF: Sorry about dinner.
HELENA: It was fine. Thank you.
CLIFF: Well, everyone seems to be leaving. (*To* ALISON) You
    packed?
ALISON: Yes.
CLIFF: Staying with Ron?
ALISON: Till Jimmy's case comes up.
CLIFF: Pity he didn't blow up that People's Mother and
    Children abortion in the shopping centre. J.P.'s quite right
    for once. You can't have much respect for the people if you
    think that's what they deserve.
HELENA: Are you off too?
CLIFF: Tomorrow. The real world calls. Pressing, urgent
    problems have to be faced, lived with, not just endured.
HELENA: He'll be on his own.
CLIFF: He's accustomed to that, I'd say.
HELENA: Well, he'll have Teddy.
CLIFF: Hope he doesn't invite Ron in. He's one of those people
    who are funny in their absence. Their presence is only
    tolerable. Think I'll light the lamp. Pity old Hugh's not
    over here.
HELENA: The famous friend who lives in California?
CLIFF: Well, mostly.
HELENA: He's not exactly *famous*, is he?
CLIFF: To a few hundred people I suppose he is. Famous but
    unsuccessful. Somehow, he manages to carry on. A subject
    of interminable speculation and bafflement. He's very
    gifted but no one is quite sure what the gift might be. In

77

Hollywood, he's feared, despised, the producer of fairly spectacular flops, he's a kind of fireball of intelligent tastelessness. J.P. is *still* perplexed at his leaving England. But there was no place for him here. I've not see him for years. He's adopted a quite ludicrous American accent – not unlike Christopher Isherwood's. They've got no ear at all out there but even they find it bizarre. It sounds as if it might be quite painful to sustain, like J.P. speaking without breathing. He's never in London more than twenty-four hours. The captain has to dash up to town if he wants to see him before Hugh becomes stricken with the idea that the country that spawned him may have insidiously poisoned him or defiled him in his hotel bedroom. No, he'd never come up to the Midlands. He got out all those years ago, leaving J.P. to face the advancing Birnham Wood of three-piece suites and Hugh's mocking voice saying, 'What did you expect?'

(*He strikes a match, about to light the oil lamp, when a shadowy figure appears in the wrong part of the kitchen. It emerges swiftly into sight, wearing a black balaclava, a raincoat and pointing a sporting rifle. They look at it for a few seconds, then the flame from the match burns* CLIFF'*s finger and he retreats from the lamp. The figure points the rifle slowly and deliberately at him, raises it, aims it and looks about to fire. Then it throws the rifle at* CLIFF, *who catches it somehow. The figure whips off the balaclava. It is* J.P., *who sings immediately:*)

J.P.: There's a little devil dancin'
    In your laughing Irish eyes . . .*

(*When* CLIFF *has recovered from his undoubted shock after a few moments he looks down at the rifle and approaches* J.P. *in genuine anger.*)

CLIFF: You imbecile! You absurd obscene imbecile! You pillock Porter! You nearly gave me a heart attack. You did! You really did.

*For full lyrics, see page 104.

J.P.: Of course, I didn't. You wouldn't be fooled by a cheap trick like that. The girls weren't, were you?

CLIFF: How do you know they weren't? How could you be sure? Talk about El Cheapo. It's not even an unfunny joke to me.

J.P.: Nonsense.

(*He continues to sing in the exaggerated style of an old Irish tenor.* CLIFF *is still not quite recovered and starts hitting him around the chest and shoulders.*)

CLIFF: You moron. Just because I'm dumb enough to fall for your cheap, pointless tricks.

(J.P. *tries to control him, embracing him, attempting to dance with him, breaking into:*)

J.P.: When Irish eyes are smiling
      Sure it's like a morn in spring.

CLIFF: Fuck you!

J.P.: Come. Sushdie.

CLIFF: Fuck you, you poor, washed-up, bloody inconsiderate maniac. Playing silly buggers with people's lives.

(*As their scuffling begins to subside,* ALISON *lets out a cry of rage, walks over to Teddy, grabs him, opens the mouth of the Aga and suspends him over it. The two men stop almost immediately and look at* HELENA. *She applauds lightly.* CLIFF *moves rather uncertainly to the smoking Teddy and rescues him. As* ALISON *moves to go:*)

J.P.: Just a moment. Here. (*He produces a red and white football supporter's woolly cap and scarf.*) We mustn't let young Jim depart without his colours. Not if he's to pursue his present occupation.

(*He pulls the cap on her head and places the scarf around her neck.*)

Caparisoned thus: he will surely never walk alone. Don't you think?

(ALISON *goes out.*)

HELENA: You've no concern at all, have you?

J.P.: Concern? The busybody's gin – demonstrably not.

(HELENA *follows* ALISON *out.* CLIFF *mops Teddy down with a drying cloth and sits at the table.* J.P. *pours them both some*

79

wine, then goes to the window. A car door is slammed, outside.)

Well, they're all gone.

CLIFF: Fancy.

J.P.: You tomorrow?

CLIFF: That's right.

J.P.: Back to the real world.

CLIFF: It may be paved with cant and complaining. But no one tries to scare me to death.

J.P.: I had a card from Hugh the other day.

CLIFF: Yes?

J.P.: Doing a location recce for some television film, in some one-man, one-vote new democracy.

CLIFF: One man, one vote. The one man's the president and *he's* got the vote. I know. What did he say?

J.P.: Usual. Why don't I get out of this dead dreary land and come somewhere like this new, emerging country. I've been talking with the president. *With* the president.

CLIFF: I'm afraid you'll have to get used to that. Especially from Hugh.

(HELENA *appears.*)

HELENA: Used to what?

CLIFF: The fact that it's not 1956 any longer for a start. He didn't like that either. You wouldn't remember. After all this silly bugger's scrum, I'm going to watch something soothing and beautiful: the Wales–France match. (CLIFF *goes.*)

HELENA: Alison told me to tell you she's sorry about Teddy.

J.P.: She was quite right. He's not at all interesting. I think he must go. Characteristically, he's already turned it to advantage. He's starting Abused Teddy Action Concern. Or is it Teddy-Line? Drink?

HELENA: I don't think so. They tell me you used to play the trumpet.

J.P.: For a while.

HELENA: Alison says you were very good.

J.P.: She can't remember. The Gatling gun of the guitar had mastered the world long before she was born.

HELENA: Don't you *ever* play it?

J.P.: Oh, on my own now and then. My old dog didn't like it too much. Before, it used to annoy the neighbours. Now I don't have any neighbours. My dog's gone but there's still the wild life. I shouldn't pollute the environment for *them*, should I? (*He opens a cupboard and takes out a case, places it on the table and takes out a trumpet, giving it a polish or two with his handkerchief.*) Anyway, I lost my puff. And it didn't seem an appropriate sound any longer. You really wouldn't enjoy it at all.

HELENA: No?

J.P.: No.

HELENA: Why not try me? There's no one here.

J.P.: I'm out of practice. Are you getting the train?

HELENA: Yes.

J.P.: I'll take you in.

HELENA: I've ordered a taxi.

J.P.: Very sensible . . . If I promise not to sing or tell jokes – would you delay your departure? Slightly? You'd be quite safe.

HELENA: I know.

J.P.: You're quite right. I'm very tired and you're very young. Irony. That English virtue that purifies our rowdy passion . . . (*Handles the trumpet.*) You wouldn't care for this – not ever . . .

HELENA: You've really fucked up your life, haven't you?

J.P.: Yes . . . With a little help. But it's not quite over yet. (*Looks at the wine.*) Shall we finish this? Oh, it's almost dead. (*He pours out the remainder. Pause.*)

HELENA: You could open another.

J.P.: (*Raising his glass*) My old dog had the best idea. To caprice.

HELENA: To brave causes. Ecce il leone!

(*They drink. J.P. goes to window, his back to audience. Then he starts, tentatively, to play 'Lead, Kindly Light' or, perhaps, 'Just a Closer Walk with Thee'. J.P. winces at this, goes and snaps on the tape recorder – 'Tornami a vagheggiar' from Handel's Alcina. A superb female voice seems to come from*

81

him as he mimes the aria, first front, then to her. He coaxes her to her feet, putting his arm around her. Amused a little, she moves with him, then slaps his face mockingly. In return, he kisses her lightly but warmly, as the orchestra takes over from his mime . . . Blackout.)

ACT THREE

SCENE I

The same. CLIFF *and* J.P. *are seated in their respective armchairs.* HELENA *is standing behind the ironing board. She wears a T-shirt inscribed with the words* J.P. IS SCUM, OK. *Teddy is wearing a bandage.*

J.P.: (*Presently*) Why do I –
CLIFF: No. Please not . . .
J.P.: Yes. It *was* a stupefyingly stupid question.
CLIFF: No more questions.
J.P.: No more *answers*.
CLIFF: You never had any.
J.P.: Never. I don't think I ever tried to stop anyone doing anything.
CLIFF: Erase the past. Right, Helena?
HELENA: Not so difficult. In my case.
J.P.: Don't miss what you've never had. Or thought you never had.
HELENA: You seem in a dull mood. Both of you.
CLIFF: I know. Come on, J.P. Sparkle a bit!
J.P.: *You* sparkle. Helena: sparkle.
(*Pause.*)
(*Noël Coward delivery*) I went round the world, you know.
CLIFF: How was that?
J.P.: The world? Developing.
CLIFF: And you? And have *you* developed?
J.P.: Not at all. Still, ultimately and finally a futile gesture.
CLIFF: Well, you can't repeat each cheap, easy success.
J.P.: No return bouts for El Cheapo. Why am I so modest, Whittaker?
CLIFF: You have every reason.
J.P.: Indeed, why did I not learn the art of immodesty?
CLIFF: You could have had two shows of your own on telly. Been an MP demanding inquiries.

83

J.P.: I do. I demand an inquiry. Good God, no I don't. Hand
me the other one.

(CLIFF *does so*.)

CLIFF: Teddy's concerned –

J.P.: *I* thought there was going to be a moratorium on Teddy.
All right then, let's get it over. What's the latest from the
Ursine Rialto?

CLIFF: For one thing: he's concerned about the North–South
divide.

J.P.: Tell him to forget it. He's in the Midlands.

CLIFF: Ah, but what about his *position*?

J.P.: Let him look to his infrastructure. It looks pretty ropey to
me.

CLIFF: Yes, but do you think it makes a *statement*?

J.P.: Is it necessary?

CLIFF: Oh, it does. Particularly as he is caught in the poverty
trap.

J.P.: Oh, a cardboard case, is he?

CLIFF: Well, not exactly. Yet. But he is dependent on your
charity. Which is demeaning.

J.P.: Perhaps he should spend less on guzzling all those nasty
buns?

CLIFF: Instead of making a cheap, wholesome soup out of stock
and vegetables. What do you take him for? A peasant?

J.P.: He doesn't work, so I suppose he can't be.

CLIFF: He can't eat wholesome food. Capitalist society has seen
to that. No, this is a matter of laying down first principles.
What's required in our changing society is a Teddy's
Charter.

J.P.: Indubitably.

CLIFF: But he needs your support.

J.P.: Counselling?

CLIFF: More. You see, our Ted has an astute mind *but* he's a
poor communicator.

J.P.: So am I. Nobody understands a word I say.

HELENA: Telling me.

CLIFF: But you're privileged. How can he even contemplate
bringing young bears into the world?

J.P.: Tell him – don't.

CLIFF: There's the pressing question of Fathers' Rights. What guarantee does he have?

J.P.: He wants to be rewarded for being a father? *And* being a Teddy?

CLIFF: Well, it's quite clear to me. He should take his case to the European Court of Teddy Rights. He would like a lively debate.

J.P.: You did say he was astute.

CLIFF: *But* he still lacks training in relationship skills. Don't pretend you can't see that, J.P. He *must* be encouraged to work out control techniques for his compulsive tendencies and evolve a suitable ethic for his individual needs and culture. Can't you bring yourself to talk to him?

J.P.: Not if I have to endure his finger-painting, sandpit culture.

CLIFF: Our society does nothing but place outmoded obstacles in his path.

J.P.: Couldn't he drop concrete blocks on a few intransigent cancer patients *en route* for the chemotherapy department?

CLIFF: I shall ignore that attempt at bad taste.

J.P.: I try my little best.

CLIFF: He wants to *participate*. That's why he's become such a totally convinced Euro-European.

J.P.: Activated, orientated, motivated –

CLIFF: He won't be put down by the likes of you any longer. No, that's why he's hopeful at this moment in time, at the end of the day, of learning the languages of the future: French, German, Urdu, Bengali, Gujerati, Hebrew . . . Welsh.

J.P.: Well, tell him to wash his mouth out afterwards.

CLIFF: He already has a firm grasp of New York Jewish humour and the international role of comedy in film –

J.P.: Oh yes, supporting wild life.

CLIFF: Damn it, J.P., he's only human –

J.P.: Damn *you*, that's just what he's not. It's what he's been told.

CLIFF: All he wants is to learn.

J.P.: His own way, you mean –

CLIFF: To create a better and more just society –

J.P.: Teddy on board. Keep your distance. Above all, like children, he must be dissuaded from any, but any, forms of self-expression. Those can be contained in the form filling for whatever happens to be his favourite method of self-help-yourself.

CLIFF: You know, J.P., I really had come to believe that you had mellowed. Everybody says so.

J.P.: I am. Mellow, mellow, sere and yellow, a mushy, over-ripe and sleepy pear.

CLIFF: No. You're not. I was mistaken. You're bad. You're giving out very bad vibes. And it's very noticeable.

J.P.: Well, my free and everlasting vibe for Teddy and all his kind is simple. I wouldn't give him the sweat from my balls. Now –

CLIFF: What about some more Nicaraguan '89?

J.P.: You know where it is. My feet hurt.

CLIFF: Try washing your socks. This is quite good. Pity Alison's not here.

(HELENA *looks half-comically distraught.*)

HELENA: Which one?

J.P.: I'll shut up in a minute.

CLIFF: Please.

J.P.: Hallelujah. Am I doing . . .

CLIFF: Not quite yet.

J.P.: These braces are a frightful mistake. Sorry, Helena. I look like an executive.

HELENA: No. You don't actually.

J.P.: Ah 'actually' – try and put *that* in Croatian. Here we are. 'This Sunday Janey Proudfoot opens her heart for the first time.' Hope Alison won't start opening her heart. '"I've learned to minimize my stress," says Janey, forty-one, playing with her cottage-cheese salad and sipping Perrier.' Forty-one! Blimey, she was our age when we were contravening the Street Traders Act of 1956. '"Acting is indispensable to my personality. My work is filled with challenges and constantly having to communicate."'

CLIFF: She's been reading again.

J.P.: Have you ever seen any of this woman's films?

HELENA: Can't say I have.

J.P.: '"As an actress, sensuality and eroticism are something that I forge consciously."' It is, she says, a structured approach. Hear that, Teddy? '"Are you still vulnerable?" I asked. "Good God, yes. Everyone is. The difference is that I'm prepared to admit it. When I act, the danger and the fear are there until the day I die. I use my men as buffers against the world. I call it keeping Janey safe. The trouble with becoming famous is your getting immersed in a complicated world of possessions, power and success. But I have many beautiful people working for me who have climbed the ladder of success with me. I don't want to be lonely up there with my celebrity. It can be so troublesome." She mentioned to her manager that it was time to go, rattling her discreet jewellery at me. "She really does go straight for it," he said. And she has no ego, which is a rare thing.'

CLIFF: Blimey!

J.P.: 'She turned to go and all eyes in the room swivelled towards us. She held out her hand in farewell. "I am into personal growth," she said.'

HELENA: Silly bitch.

CLIFF: What's on the telly?

J.P.: Wales versus France. We don't want that.

CLIFF: Speak for yourself.

J.P.: What a gift from Zeus. Never to be bored by yourself. Only by others. Alison was never happier since she set out to become an actress. I bored her.

CLIFF: You did, captain. You did.

J.P.: Everybody bored her. Same with my daughter's mama. After she's extracted their own unique little piece of distinction or fame from someone and shot it up into her own system, it's on to the next. Every day brings a new baby seal to be lamented.

CLIFF: One thing, Porter, you were never a baby seal.

HELENA: Were you never bored with *them*?

J.P.: Oh, yes.

HELENA: You talk about them enough.

J.P.: (*Light, almost musical-comedy vein*) They are my pestilential years. How *can* I disregard them? Besides, I never had their godlike gift. A system of immunity to any later opportunity of self-boredom. What it must be to stand up and say, 'I am into personal growth.' If God were to make actresses and politicians of us all, borne aloft on the clouds of self-delight!

CLIFF: What's on?

J.P.: What have we here? Entertainment. What to watch out for. Well: the Hollywood star Perkin Schwarzkopf is to make an appearance in a new West End production of *King Lear*. 'Typical of his artistic approach to each part he plays, Perkin researched the role by living as an inmate in an old people's home for five months and underwent at least three weeks of enforced feeding and incontinence.' There's a box-office advance of £700,000 for the limited season. Ah, yes, on Good Friday the Great Midlands Leisure Complex is presenting a rock version of *Messiah*. A man of sorrow and acquainted with grief becomes a disoriented guy uncounselled in his stress. Top DJ Keith Katz says, 'Old GFH would have loved it! After all, he was the great pop musician of his day.' Several prominent churchmen enthusiastically agree, including –

CLIFF: The Rev. Ron.

J.P.: Wait for it. The –

CLIFF: Bishop of Bromley.

J.P.: Who says it makes the Christian message meaningful for young people in a pulsing idiom of today. 'After all, what is Christianity but the story of the one-parent family?'

CLIFF: He said what!

J.P.: I do not have the facility or energy for inventions. Why bother with art when every man's his own surrealist?

CLIFF: Perhaps we should go.

HELENA: I've booked tickets for you both.

CLIFF: There's a lady here says there's no such thing as a lesbian Tory.

J.P.: Blimey, she should come and live here. One ex-major, a sergeant and two ex-WAFs, the riding-school lady, a retired industrial psychologist and one joint MFH.

CLIFF: And that's just in the village. They all seem to like *me*.

HELENA: Why shouldn't they?

CLIFF: Why should they?

J.P.: If life's been hard on them, they don't blame it on J.P. Dominant Male Esquire.

CLIFF: You're about as dominant as Minnie Mouse.

J.P.: I was always a baby seal at heart. What are *you* smirking about?

CLIFF: I was just thinking of Janey in heaven.

J.P.: Yes. Down-on-your-Left, Saint Peter. At least she's a non-smoker.

CLIFF: That should get her in.

J.P.: You say I'm negative, all gripe and no solutions. What *about* Young Folk's Homes? Pre-retirement homes for Junior Citizens? Senility is institutionalized. Why not adolescence?

HELENA: You don't like anyone, do you?

J.P.: Yes. But I may get round to it.

HELENA: *You* were never an adolescent?

J.P.: I wasn't a teenager.

CLIFF: They were before his time.

J.P.: Nor middle-aged. My school was stuffed with executives in short trousers already pining for their pensions. Missed both stages. It says here –

CLIFF: That's enough of that.

J.P.: 'Sir Anthony Wills, our foremost theatrical administrator and champion of the arts, admits freely to being a lifelong workaholic.' How disgusting. Admitting openly to work abuse.

CLIFF: What will *he* get up to in heaven?

J.P.: Chuck *my* money at a lot of no-talent con-persons. A superb politician – Politician! He looks like Guy Fawkes and they think he's smooth and subtle, is at his desk at 6 a.m. seven days a week, hates holidays . . . I can't bear it!

CLIFF: What's on the telly? Why can't you lead a full and useful life like that? Give it here.

J.P.: Well, let's have something cheerful, ducks. I've never really believed in these braces. They need restructuring. Like a dead and alive hole like this place. Well, I've had quite enough upsets in my life, I can't stand any more. Yes. Well, you don't want any more, do you? *You've* had your share as well, haven't you?

CLIFF: I have.

(HELENA *leaves the ironing board and looks out of the window. A depressive mood is descending on all of them.*)

J.P.: Nemmind, duck. God pays debts without money.

CLIFF: That's right.

J.P.: *I've* never owed anybody anything.

CLIFF: You haven't, no.

J.P.: I was always an honest person.

CLIFF: You were.

J.P.: Always. Never owed anybody nothing. Still, they don't care, do they? They don't –

CLIFF: They certainly don't.

J.P.: It's a funny old world, innit?

CLIFF: That's right.

J.P.: Wouldn't do if we was all the same, would it?

CLIFF: My God. No.

J.P.: Still, it makes you think.

CLIFF: It does.

J.P.: Sometimes I sit on the toilet. They've still done nothing about that glass pane in my toilet.

CLIFF: No?

J.P.: I've written to the council.

CLIFF: They won't do nothing.

J.P.: 'Course they won't. Nobody cares about us.

CLIFF: This Government wants hanging if you ask me.

J.P.: Too good for 'em – eh? (*Chuckles.*) No, I sit on the toilet of a morning and I say to myself, 'Jim.'

CLIFF: Yes?

J.P.: You've got nothing to reproach yourself for. You can always hold your head up. Yes, you can. You know that time I was in hospital? Five operations I had.

CLIFF: Five.

J.P.: Five operations. And do you know – I always got to a vessel.

CLIFF: Always.

J.P.: Even Alison's mother remembers that. That time at Auntie Eva's when she was going on. I reminded her. You could write a play about me, you could.

CLIFF: You could.

J.P.: Can't help laughing though, can you?

CLIFF: No.

J.P.: Uncle Hugh, he always liked a nice play.

CLIFF: He did, didn't he?

J.P.: Oh yes . . . We all did. In *them* days.

CLIFF: Them days. Yes.

J.P.: Everybody did. Well, now you're talking, aren't you? Lots of music and dancing in them days. Real music. Don't get that now.

CLIFF: No. Not now.

J.P.: Just a lot of noise.

CLIFF: That's right.

(HELENA *returns wearily to the ironing board.*)

That was very depressing.

J.P.: It was.

CLIFF: I thought Helena had bucked you up a bit.

J.P.: She had.

(CLIFF *looks over to her for the first time and takes her in at the ironing board.*)

CLIFF: Good God!

J.P.: What?

CLIFF: What's she doing?

J.P.: Doing?

CLIFF: *Doing?*

(J.P. *looks round.*)

J.P.: What do you think? Ironing, of course.

CLIFF: That's your shirt. *Your* shirt.

J.P.: My dear Whittaker. My dear Whittaker, you chose the perfect profession. You respond to nothing but reportage and shared revelations. To you that wooden object is a bygone symbol of woman's drudgery. You can't detect the whiff of burnt ironies given off by a mere ironing board. Young Helena told me, when she was a proud sixteen, she vowed that she would never be prevailed upon or coaxed into the degradation of ironing a man's shirt. Since then no desperate entreaty has moved her heart to break that supreme commandment.

CLIFF: Don't tell me *you* moved her heart.

J.P.: May God in heaven forfend. We came to an agreement.

CLIFF: You mean you'd stop fooling around? All that gabble and songs.

J.P.: That we'd pretend we were both human beings.

CLIFF: And you succeeded.

J.P.: *She* did. Triumphantly.

CLIFF: I'm sure. But what about you?

J.P.: Well, she's ironing my shirt, isn't she?

CLIFF: You've a hidden spring of generosity, all right.

HELENA: Call it a one-off caprice.

J.P.: The first and last. Never again, eh?

HELENA: That's right. There you are, one shirt. Male. Somewhat flailing. For the use of.

J.P.: Thank you. Very much. I shall not wear this shirt. It shall be kept in tissue in a drawer of memories. Smell it, Whittaker, fresh and Edwardian crisp, as from an Italian countrywoman's sunny basket.

CLIFF: What's *your* symbolic gesture then?

J.P.: I've run out of those. They won't wash. When you've no expectations, the most faint and distant chimes peal out like victory.

CLIFF: It won't last.

J.P.: The blood is up again. I'll take you both out to dinner.

HELENA: I'm catching the evening train.

J.P.: No matter. I'll sing you a song.

CLIFF: No. You promised.

(J.P. *folds up the ironing board ceremoniously, finally leaning on it.*)

J.P.: Porter's the name. My spirits worsen
    Believed to be a fucked-up person
    Pursued by bullies up the creek

I migrate in sorrow. Once a week.
(*He taps a button on the tape recorder.*)
CLIFF: You've made him *worse*.
(J.P., *assisted by the ironing board, hops on to a chair and sings to the tune of the Champagne Aria from* Don Giovanni:)
J.P.: Here stands Jimmy Porter,
    Abused his son and only daughter,
    Raped the lives of luckless wives,
    Said sexist things he didn't oughter,
    His one and only paltry function,
    Providing prigs with holy unction.
    Said racist things he didn't oughter,
    His one and only paltry function,
    Providing prigs with holy unction.
(CLIFF *turns off the tape.*)
CLIFF: That must have wasted a few hours.
(*Phone from outer kitchen rings.*)
J.P.: I'll get it. (*He goes.*)
CLIFF: God. He's reconnected to the world. You're off then?
HELENA: You didn't think I was staying, did you? And you?
CLIFF: In the morning.
HELENA: How *does* he manage?
CLIFF: Now then, Helena. It was never explained *why* he ran a sweet stall, remember. I think old first father-in-law, the Colonel, settled a small sum. Intended as a secret. It sure toppled old Mummy Rhino into the grave. You know how sacred wills and entails are to those people. That must have been a one-off caprice too. One more stereotype fighting back.
(*Enter* J.P.)
Hello, whitey. Blimey, you *are* white. I was telling her about the Colonel.
(J.P. *goes to the fridge and takes out a bottle of champagne.*)
J.P.: He was a good old stick. Well, he was very nice to me, which is the yardstick we judge all people by, I suppose. After Alison left, I always got a Christmas card from him with just the initial R. Before the battalion band played him off to the smokeless regimental mess above. (*Opens the*

93

champagne and pours three glasses.) Here's to him. He had all the patrician qualities: remoteness, detachment and magnanimity. Hugh was the same. Remoteness, especially. Here's to them both.

CLIFF: You look awful. Really past it.

J.P.: I am. And to the living. You, Helena. The Brave New – something very much.

CLIFF: What do you mean: Hugh was the same?

J.P.: You're not the only one whose father was a man. You're doing quite well. Hugh died in his sleep this morning. Gone to Captain Shanks and my dear old dog.

HELENA: I'm sorry.

CLIFF: What was it?

J.P.: What does it matter?

CLIFF: I knew it was a bad idea, you answering the phone.

J.P.: Something mysterious, I expect, knowing Hugh. Remote to the last. Ned, (*To* HELENA) his son, wasn't very coherent.

CLIFF: Was he upset?

J.P.: Very. I told him to come up here. He's my godson. Hugh was never keen on the idea, but we agreed finally. Ned's father always denigrated him. The daughter was his favourite for some perverse reason. Complacent, tight-arsed little package but Hugh adored her. Ned's different.

HELENA: Less remote?

J.P.: He actually likes it *here*.

HELENA: Unlike your own children.

J.P.: He doesn't throw up at the sight of a little mess of muddled enthusiasm.

HELENA: He'll cry at the dog's burial?

J.P.: You can *all* go, please, all of you.

CLIFF: (*Rises*) I'll go back to Twickenham. (*Like TV reporter*) How are you feeling now that your best friend is dead?

J.P.: I wish to be alone in my personal disasters.

CLIFF: (*To* HELENA) He'll be in need of some bereavement counselling. (*He goes.*)

J.P.: You'd better get your train. We don't want to tarnish our restrained little interlude. Cliff will take you to the station.

94

HELENA: You haven't learnt anything about me, have you?

J.P.: Hardly a thing.

HELENA: Did you expect to?

J.P.: No. I don't know much less than I do about my children, their mother. My ex-wife. I look for a glimpse of pleasure not enlightenment. Look at Teddy, he's quite a jolly little sphinx if you've a whimsical bent. But his secret's not worth the probing. I've looked for secrets where there were none. Everyone demands solutions, like happiness, as their right. You go to sleep at night and wake up with the same old *Giaconda* frown beside you. (*Sings to the tune 'Amapola':*)

> Giaconda, my smiling Giaconda,
> I like to watch and wonder,
> I know I'll never get beyond its empty mystery.

I thought my first wife was concealing something. Something to declare *there*, I thought. Now she does, of course. To the whole world. I've no secrets. But I'm sometimes in the market for them. Like old T. Bear there. That's why he keeps changing his dumb little mind and it runs ever the same. Well, this won't buy the baby a new bonnet.

> Replete of sin, devoid of guilt,
> For holocaust I never built
> A cheery, unrepentant sod,
> Mine's an ad hoc relationship with God.

HELENA: (*Rising*) Well, I hope your new relationship with young Ned is a helpful one. For both of you. You've really become an awful unholy bloody clown, haven't you?
(*She kisses him on the forehead.*)

J.P.: Clowns don't laugh.
(*She goes to the door.*)
Oh, Helena . . .
(*She turns.*)
Thank you. Thank you for ironing my shirt.
(*She leaves as he shakily pours a glass of champagne. Blackout. Music/song: possibly 'A Good Man Nowadays is Hard to Find'.*)

95

The same. Only the oil lamp is burning. Teddy wears a black armband. CLIFF *and* J.P. *in their respective armchairs.*

J.P.: (*As Private Lives*) I went round the world you know. After –
CLIFF: How was it?
J.P.: The world? Far too long.
CLIFF: Like plays.
J.P.: Either too long –
CLIFF: – or too short. Pity they don't have third acts any more.
J.P.: Quite, quite enough.
CLIFF: One does need a drink. (*Reverts to tone of last duologue:*) Ever see anything of Auntie Eva these days?
J.P.: No. Never writes. Think she'd send a postcard or something. Right opposite the post office. But never anything, not even on Alison's birthday. And she always thought the world of *her*.
CLIFF: Oh, yes, she was always the favourite.
J.P.: I was the *one* she wasn't keen on. Me.
CLIFF: Why was that I wonder?
J.P.: I never did her no harm. Still, there it is. People are funny.
CLIFF: They are.
J.P.: Don't know what gets into some of 'em. Young Jimmy. And Alison. *And* her mother. Don't know what gets into some of 'em. I don't. That poor Captain Shanks. All right one minute and then off up in the air somewhere.
CLIFF: Up in the air's right.
J.P.: Well, one thing, ducks, I know *I've* not done anything.
CLIFF: No, you 'aven't.
J.P.: My conscience is clear. Let them sort it out themselves.
CLIFF: That's the ticket.
J.P.: I'm not bothered any longer. Time comes when they can't hurt you no longer.

CLIFF: Can't hurt you no more.

J.P.: They can't.

CLIFF: However much they go on.

J.P.: Can't hurt you. Not any longer. Isn't that right?

CLIFF: That's right.

J.P.: Nemmind, eh, ducks?

CLIFF: Nemmind, eh, Ted?

J.P.: After all, what am I?

CLIFF: You're a cunt.

J.P.: I'm a contraflow.

CLIFF: Pour me some more wine.

J.P.: (*Rises to pour drink.*) I am a young couple, a young executive . . .

CLIFF: You're pissed.

J.P.: (*Rattles off*) . . . waiting twelve hours at the airport; I am a baggage handler on strike. I am a survey, an infrastructure; a mortgage wrapped about my inability to have an orgasm; I am a steamer, a government statistic, a gymslip mother; I am a Walkman with an inalienable right to hope and happiness and rights; above all I am Right, to work, to guidelines, I am a grand object of public unconcern, an unscheduled delay, a workshop of new attitudes and ideas; the sounding brass of pop and charity, the rattle and the scarf, the boot, the Arts Council, banality and yoof; *Civis Britannicus* scum. Finally: I still am, after thirty years, a churlish, grating note, a spokesman for no one but myself; with deadening effect, cruelly abusive, unable to be coherent about my despair; uncomfortable and awkward. His only response a cynical guffaw. No real motivation, lashing out wildly in all directions, never identifying the shadows he is attacking. *We* are left to work out our own causes; futility is our only clue. Is this ugly, cheerless world supposed to be typical? By no means an artistic success despite some violent knockabout here and there. But, my friends, finally, finally and in the last examination, the total –

CLIFF: – gesture is –

J.P. *and* CLIFF: (*Together*) Altogether Inadequate.

J.P.: And has remained so for thirty years. Perhaps, wait for it, *next* time –

CLIFF: *Next* time he will let us *know what* he is angry about . . .
Pretty *déjàvu*. I'd say. You're still a cunt. You are –
become very cold, Father Porter . . . the young Teddy
said. And you're becoming increasingly cold.

J.P.: If I am cold, it is the cold that burns . . .
(*Pause.*)

CLIFF: Who's that?

J.P.: Who's what?
(*There is the sound of a car coming up the drive outside. It
stops.*)
How do I know? Go and have a look.

CLIFF: Go yourself.

J.P.: I'm insufficiently motivated.

CLIFF: Oh, hell. (*He gets up to the window and peers out.*)

J.P.: Well – can't be anything good, can it? It's Vatman come
for Teddy. (*To* TEDDY) Well, you would go into Europe.
Now they've come for you. It's all that champagne he
sloshes down his little socialist throat. Well, pay the man
and you'll feel so much better.

CLIFF: It's the Rev. Ron.

J.P.: Well, he can fuck off back to St Bleeding Heart's and the
liturgical leisure centre at once.

CLIFF: Someone's getting out.

J.P.: He can't think he's come to the Inner City. Actually, he
has.

CLIFF: It's Alison. She's taking out a suitcase . . . She's back,
James. Why don't you meet her at the door? Go on.

J.P.: We don't want to frighten her off. Do we?

CLIFF: You don't?

J.P.: I'm still dumb enough to believe in divinely flexible
heroines. You go.

CLIFF: Be nice.

J.P.: I'm always nice. Tell the Rev. Ron we've got double
glazing, and it doesn't work.

CLIFF: I shall be sickeningly polite.

J.P.: And tell her Ned's coming. To stay. That'll please her.

CLIFF: (*At door*) I wish you'd go yourself.

J.P.: Say I'm in here. Preparing the prodigal's baked meats.
(CLIFF *goes.* J.P. *goes to the fridge excitedly and produces a bottle of champagne, deciding between a Moët and a Dom Perignon. He chooses the latter. He glances out of the window hurriedly, picks up* TEDDY *and places him on the table to face the door and places Alison's personal stereo ear-pieces on his head. There is the sound of voices and laughter from the hall. He opens the bottle and pours three glasses, then rifles through a pile of tapes on the sideboard, selects one and puts it in the machine. It is a fairly standard pop number. He grimaces and turns the volume down a little, then, standing expectantly at the Aga – to which he makes the sign of the Cross – he begins to fill his pipe. Smoke pours forth from him as he waits. Presently,* CLIFF *enters. He looks across at* J.P., *then, turning off the tape player, he settles back into his armchair.*)

J.P.: Champagne?

CLIFF: Thanks. I could do with that.
(J.P. *hands him one of the three glasses, takes one for himself and moves slowly to the window and looks out. There is the sound of car doors slamming, voices, then the car moving off. Silence.* CLIFF *waits for a while before he speaks.*)
She's left behind some of her records.

J.P.: Oh, yes?

CLIFF: Oh, and her personal stereo.

J.P.: Teddy's using it.

CLIFF: Yes. Well, I said you'd send it on.

J.P.: Of course.
(*He places the third glass of champagne in front of* TEDDY.)
Cheers.

CLIFF: Cheers . . . What?

J.P.: I didn't say anything.
(*Pause.*)

CLIFF: What do you think – young Jim will do after his community service?

J.P.: I don't know . . .

CLIFF: Do you think Alison will have an abortion?

J.P.: I've no idea. How was she looking?

CLIFF: Terrific. Shouldn't you find out?

J.P.: Why?

CLIFF: I should have thought pride was a bit LMC for you.

J.P.: I've no pride. Just a distaste for piety.

CLIFF: Well, there is –

J.P.: Young Ned will need my attention. He'll be upset about the dog. Envy? I was too arrogant. Gluttony? Certainly not. I refused to queue and despised second helpings. Avarice?

CLIFF: No.

J.P.: Thanks, Whittaker. Wrath? Oh, not as much as people thought. Lust? Now and then. Mostly then. Sloth? Oh, yes, most certainly and grievously. Sloth.

CLIFF: My feet hurt . . .

J.P.: You've said that already . . . (*He picks up his trumpet and opens the window.*)

CLIFF: Have I? Sorry, I'm sure.

J.P.: Keep thou my feet, I do not ask to see
      The distant scene; one step enough for me.
      (*Puts the trumpet to his lips.*) I was not ever thus. (*He plays, uncertainly at first, 'Lead, Kindly Light'.*)

CLIFF: I loved to choose and see my path but now –
      (*Trumpet louder.*)
      – lead thou me on.

J.P.: (*Stops*) I loved the garish day, and spite of fears
      Pride ruled my will; remember not past years.
      (*He plays on.*)

CLIFF: The night is dark and I am far from home.
      Sure it still leads me on,
      And with the moon those angel voices smile,
      Which I have loved long since and lost awhile.
      (*Presently* J.P. *stops playing and listens. The church bells peal out suddenly.*)
      Those bloody bells!

J.P.: (*By the window sill*) Give us leave to depart the perils of this night.

CLIFF: Stop those bloody bells!

J.P.: So that we may awake watchfully.

CLIFF: Close the window.

J.P.: Even in our pestilence and squalor renew our powers against the armies of the strident and self-righteous.

CLIFF: The Rev. Ron wouldn't go for that.

J.P.: And against the noise and clamour of those who would impose their certainties upon us. God *rot* their certainties.

CLIFF: That's more like it, Cornet.

J.P.: (*Very crisply, like battle commands*) Endow us with the courage of uncertainty. Accept an unruly but contrite heart. And in that frailty of disbelief we cannot overcome let us seek remedy from within ourselves and offer mercy that the world cannot give among the perils etcetera, etcetera.

CLIFF: Amen. Teddy didn't like it. Teddy doesn't –

J.P.: Doesn't what?

CLIFF: Sorry. Teddy doesn't understand why it is that God allows so much suffering. In the world.

J.P.: He goes really straight to the heart of it, doesn't he?

CLIFF: Not when –

J.P.: When it's in his power to stop it?

CLIFF: Well, it's a fair question.

J.P.: Tell him not to come that Belsize Park smarmy sanctimony with us. 'I'd like so much to believe in God, but I'm afraid he just doesn't live up to my own moral necessities.'

CLIFF: What should I tell him?

J.P.: Tell him to go fuck himself. He didn't do his own son no favours. (*Closes window.*) He can invent his *own* bloody collects.

(*He puts the trumpet back in its case.* CLIFF *has the paper over his face.*)

(*To* TEDDY) I should settle down if I were you. Pretend it isn't happening. You're a lucky fellow. Mediocrity is a great comforter, my furry little ursine friend. And very democratic. It's all yours. Oh, *lucky* bears!

(J.P. *turns on the tape recorder. Champagne Aria. This time perhaps to a genuine recording. Eberhard Wechter. Or maybe just the orchestra. Whichever works best. Anyway,* J.P. *mimes to it, in his most ebullient fashion. At the end of it, he exits with a grand operatic flourish, the most upward theatrical inflexion he can muster.* CLIFF *lies asleep beneath the newspaper.*)

(*In the unlikely event of audience dissent at the end of the performance, the loud playing of martial music can be effective.* 'Molonello' *played by the Grenadier Guards, the quick march* 'St Patrick's Day' *or, to be more* 'European', *the* 'Radetzky'.)

IT'S MY MOTHER'S BIRTHDAY TODAY

It's my mother's birthday today,
I'm on my way with a lovely bouquet,
For me it's the happiest day,
I won't be late at the old cottage gate.

I'll greet her with a kiss,
For that I know she yearns,
And then I'll say God bless you,
Many happy returns.

Those roses will soon fade away,
But she'll know what I mean to convey,
When I say –
It's *my* mother's birthday today.

My heart is singing a happy refrain,
Blue skies are smiling above,
I'm going home to my mother again,
Off to the one that I love.

THERE'S A LITTLE DEVIL DANCIN'

There's a little devil dancin'
In your laughing Irish eyes,
And the little devil dances
Right into me heart.

There's a little bit of mischief,
In your laughing Irish eyes,
And it tells me you will give me
Such a grand surprise

Oh, I swear on me honour,
I'm a man who's a goner
And to prove what I can do,
You can put it in the papers
That the boys know, bejabers,
That I want to marry you.

But before we start romancing,
Darling, won't you put me wise
To the little devil dancin'
In your laughing Irish eyes?